About the Author

Born in Germany, Edgar Rothermich studie
graduated in 1989 with a Master's Degree
composer and music producer in Berlin an
continued his work on numerous projects i
Prophecy", "Outer Limits", "Babylon 5", "What the Bleep do we know", "Fuel", "Big Money Rustlas").

a

For the past 20 years Edgar has had a successful musical partnership with electronic music pioneer and founding Tangerine Dream member Christopher Franke. Recently in addition to his collaboration with Christopher, Edgar has been working with other artists as well as on his own projects.

December 2010 marked the release of his first two solo albums "Why Not Electronica" and "Why Not Electronica Again" followed by "Why Not Solo Piano", the first release in 2011. They are available on Amazon and iTunes.

www.DingDingMusic.com   GEM@DingDingMusic.com

About the GEM (Graphically Enhanced Manual)

What are Graphically Enhanced Manuals? They're a new type of manual with a visual approach that helps you UNDERSTAND a program, not just LEARN it. No need to read through 500 of pages of dry text explanations. Rich graphics and diagrams help you to get that "aha" effect and make it easy to comprehend difficult concepts. The Graphically Enhanced Manuals help you master a program much faster with a much deeper understanding of concepts, features and workflows in a very intuitive way that is easy to understand.

During my senior years at the University of Arts I was teaching technical courses as a tutor at the sound engineering department, and after graduation I continued my courses as a faculty member. I found that I could teach my students the technical concepts much better if I used illustrations and gave them visual representations of some difficult topics.

When I started to work for Christopher Franke I was confronted with his arsenal of synthesizers and computer programs and a large stack of manuals I had to work through. It became even clearer how important it was to have a good manual that explains the basic concepts before delving into the fine details. The poorly written manuals always started with "go to that menu, press that button and then do …"

Often an application or an electronic device has features that are not even explained in the manual. You have to figure out the functionality by trial and error. The biggest shortcoming of most manuals is that they're too text-heavy. "A picture's worth a thousand words" is my motto. Based on my experiences and sometimes frustrations I always create my own personal manuals for programs and devices that I use the most. Sometimes they're just notes of important information or summaries to quickly review at a later time and sometimes they are more elaborate papers.

In 2004 I was confronted with the same situation: Learning a new program with its big manual. After nearly 20 years of using Cubase to compose and record my music, I decided to finally switch to Logic Pro. In the process of learning that new app, I once again created my personal manuals. But when I realized how many other Logic users faced the same struggle to understand the app I decided to start making those manuals available on my website as Graphically Enhanced Manuals.

About the Formatting

Red colored text indicates keyboard shortcuts. I use the following abbreviations: **sh** (shift key), **ctr** (control key), **opt** (option key), **cmd** (command key). A plus (+) between the keys means that you have to press all those keys at the same time. **sh+opt+K** means: hold the shift and the option and the K key at the same time.

Brown colored text indicates Menu Commands with a greater sign (>) indicating submenus.
Edit > Source Media > All means "Click on the Edit Menu, scroll down to Source Media and select the submenu All.

Blue arrows indicate what happens if you click on an item or popup menu ●——————➤

About the Editor

Many thanks to Chas Ferry for editing and proofreading my manuals. <www.hollywoodtrax.com>

The manual is based on Compressor 4.0.1
ISBN-13: 978-1469901169
ISBN-10: 1469901161
Copyright © 2012 Edgar Rothermich
All rights reserved

Introduction

The red haired stepchild

Compressor was always that add-on app that never got the same love and attention as many of Apple's other, bigger flagship applications. Except for some hardcore users, not many editors have made full use of its potential. The program was even bundled with Logic Pro. But composers and audio engineers that used Logic had even less of a clue what to do with it and got scared away by all the video lingo that was unknown to most of them.

It seems that Compressor didn't even get the love it deserves from it's own creator, Apple. With the release of FCPx, a new look was introduced, dark and cool. Motion also got that new GUI (Graphical User Interface) treatment, but Compressor? Although the upgrade from Compressor 3 to Compressor 4 indicated a major step forward, not much had changed. Most of all, it still kept that gray "retro" OS9 feel. That, of course, didn't help to make the user curious to give it a second chance.

The fact that you are reading this manual is an indication that you are curious about Compressor 4 anyway. Hopefully, this manual will provide you the necessary understanding so the program will become a valuable tool in your work as a video editor, composer, or someone who is dealing with conversion of audio and video files.

What is Compressor?

Compressor is a utility app and not a full fledged production tool like FCPx or Logic Pro. It does not create content. Instead, you take existing content (source media files) and let Compressor change that Source Media File into a new Output Media File based on user defined parameters and settings, a process also known as Transcoding or Converting.

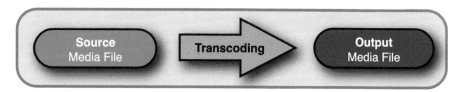

That is basically it, plain and simple. Although Compressor can get very complicated in some areas, there aren't many features to get lost in. Once you get an overview of what it can do, you can pick the areas that you need for your workflow and easily ignore other features or implement them later once your comfort level increases.

Here is an example of three different kinds of "potential" Compressor users, based on their level of experience:

➡ Casual User

A user can convert audio and video files and make use of a few simple but powerful features that are not available in iTunes or QuickTime (those apps have simple transcoding capabilities built in). Another potential use on the basic level is forced by the new FCPx. Some features in earlier FCP versions are no longer available anymore in FCPx and can now only be accomplished with Compressor (chapter markers, partial video export, etc). This forces FCP users to work with Compressor, even if they have avoided it in the past.

➡ Audio/Video Professional

On the next level, the user is pretty much familiar with most of the video parameters, simple and advanced. He takes advantage of modifying and controlling video and audio conversions down to the finest detail. On the audio level, that could mean dealing with surround file encoding.

➡ Network Administrator

For the most experienced user, Compressor provides features that are generally unfamiliar to video or audio professionals. Here we're talking about system admin territory. The components that handle those tasks were part of a separate app before (Apple Qmaster), but now they are incorporated into Compressor. However, don't let this scare you. Even if you are not a system admin for a big post production facility, you might have use for these features. With a small local network of two or three machines in your office, you can play around with that technology and see if you can use the advantage of having your own little render farm.

Terminology

First, let's get familiar with the terminology before looking at the program's user interface (GUI) and its layout. I'm introducing the different terms with step by step illustrations that show the functionality of compressor with simplified building blocks. Those building blocks represent the various elements or components in Compressor's user interface that I'll explain later.

- Here again is the basic functionality of Compressor with the three main elements:

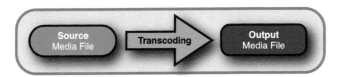

Source Media File

This is the original file that you want to change in Compressor. Please note that it is called a "Media" file. We are not talking about text files, spreadsheets or anything like that. It is kind of obvious but I thought to point it out. I discuss later what specific Media files can be transcoded in Compressor.

Transcoding

This is the heart of Compressor, the Transcoding, its main component.

Output Media File

This is the transcoded media file that Compressor creates. It is the result of the Source Media file with all the selected transcoding settings applied to it.

- Here is the same illustration with a closer look at what is "inside" the Transcoding element. It is made up of three more elements:

Settings

Settings are like Macros for specific transcoding processes, pre-defined or user-defined. They include all the instructions that determine how to alter the parameters and attributes of the Source Media File. The most important element of Compressor.

Destination

This section defines the destination for the Output Media File. In other words, in what location should Compressor store the transcoded Output Media File.

Name

Pretty much self explanatory. What name should Compressor give the new, transcoded Output Media File.

The next illustration hasn't changed. I've only added a name to the section with the three elements that make up the Transcoding. That section I called the Target.

A Target defines one single transcoding step: "Take one Source Media file and apply specific Settings+Destination+Name to create one specific Output Media File."

The next illustration also just adds another label. The new term is a *Job.*

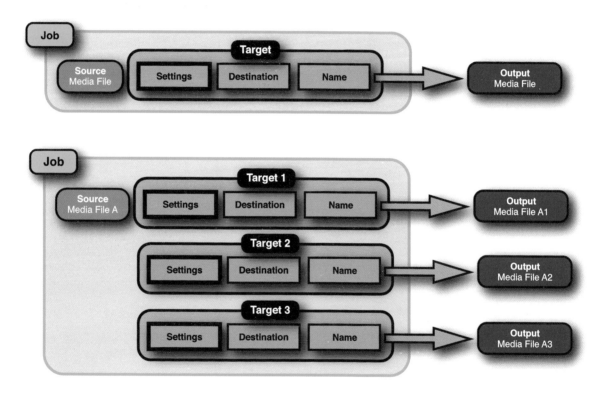

Job

A Job defines both sections: The Source Media File and the Target (which itself includes the Settings, Destination and Name element). As you can see in the second illustration, you can setup multiple Targets for the same Source Media File. For example, you could choose a Source Media File and transcode it in different ways at the same time, ending up with multiple Output Files. This way, you could transcode to a hi-def quicktime file, a smaller compressed file suitable for iPhones and upload one version to YouTube. All those instructions could be in one Job.

So a Job describes one Source Media file and one or multiple Targets.

A Job however can't exist by itself inside the Compressor application. It has to belong to a **_Batch._**

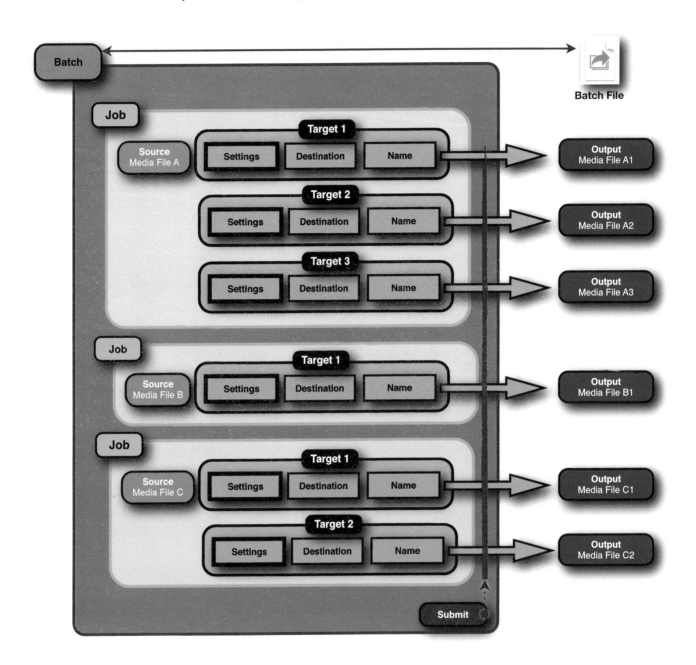

Batch File

Batch

A Batch can contain one or many Jobs. The Batch with all its configured Jobs and Targets can be saved as a Batch File to your hard drive and can be opened later in Compressor again. This way, you can set up the configuration but start the actual transcoding at a later time when the computer is sitting idle (nights or weekends).

Submit

This is the command that starts the transcoding process. Please note that you can't process a Job directly. You always process a Batch and therefore the Job(s) inside that Batch.

● Technically there is one more building block without a specific name. It is the Compressor application itself.

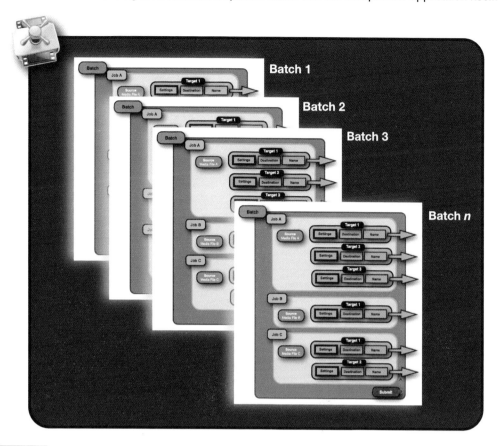

Compressor

Compressor can actually have more than one Batch open in the application, the same way a word processor can have multiple text documents open.

You can have multiple Batches open in Compressor. The only thing you have to keep in mind is that each Batch has its own Submit button which starts the transcoding process independently for that particular Batch. As we will see later, you don't have to wait for one Batch to finish processing before submitting the next one. Every transcoding job as part of a batch ends up in a queue, similar to a network printer. Think about it, a word processor app doesn't print its document once you hit the *print* command. It hands it over to the printer spooler and background app which performs the print process. This is similar to Compressor which doesn't perform the actual transcoding process. You only configure the Transcoding and the *Submit* command sends it off to the background app which performs the process. At that moment you can actually quit Compressor.

● One Transcoding Process in the big picture:

Regardless of having one or multiple transcoding jobs to do, the hierarchy is always the same. If you keep that diagram with all those elements (the building blocks) in mind, then you won't get lost when you work in the Compressor app later on. Here is an example for one single transcoding Job going through all the elements:

Open Compressor - Create a Batch (or use the default) - Create a Job (or use the default) - Select a Source Media file for that Job - Create a Target and set the desired Setting, Destination and the Name - Click Submit to start the transcoding process - the Output Media File will be created.

Standard Window Behavior

I think we should take the time to fully understand the user interface with its different windows and their behavior before we proceed any further. Then, when we dive into the detailed functionality of the transcoding Settings, we won't be distracted by the expected or unexpected behavior of some of the window elements.

Compressor is a document-based app like any other word processor or spreadsheet app. That also means that the window layout follows similar conventions.

Compressor has 6 core windows. Instead of just listing them and explaining what they do, I want to categorize them in the context of a document-based app.

Usually there are three types of windows in a document-based app and they are also found in Compressor:

- **Document Window**: This is the window that represents your document, like a text or spreadsheet document. In case of Compressor, it is the Batch Window. Each Batch that you open, is represented by a separate Batch Window.

- **Application Windows**: These are all the additional windows that are not related to a specific document window. They provide additional informations, selections or tools.

- **Linked Window**: These types of windows display information about the currently selected document window or content of another window. The Inspector Window is the most commonly used one of that type. The Preview Window in Compressor belongs to the same type. It displays the content of the currently selected Job in a Batch Window.

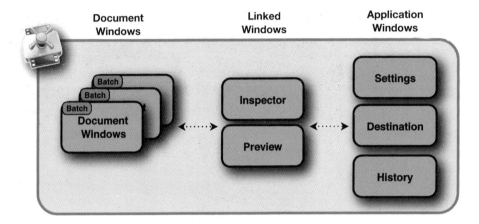

Besides those 6 core windows, there are a few more windows. They belong to advanced Compressor features or to a separate app all together:

- Apple Qmaster Sharing

- Share Monitor (separate app)

- Apple Qmaster (separate app)

The distinction of window types is important when you think about what is happening when you close a window:

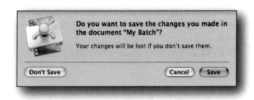

- When you close a Batch Window, you actually close that document. That means, if you've made changes to the Batch and haven't saved it as a Batch file yet, you will be prompted with an Alert window, asking you to save the Batch document.

- All other windows can be closed or opened any time.

Tabs

Compressor uses another layout convention, Tabs. This works the same way as in many web browsers. Instead of having multiple windows open that use a lot of screen real estate and get easily cluttered, you work in only one main window and have each additional windows represented by a tab that you can click to display its content in the window. Downside of course, you can view the content of only one window at a time.

Usually you would work in a mixed environment where you combine windows as tabs in a main window but tear them off as a separate window when you need to view the content of two windows side by side.

Compressor's Window Behavior

Now that we are aware of the basic window layout behavior, we will see that Apple implements those techniques in Compressor in a bit confusing way. But once we recognize those inconsistencies (or bugs), we won't be distracted by that strange window behavior and can focus on our workflow.

This is how the window Layout looks when you open Compressor the first time. What looks like one big window is actually 5 windows attached to each other in a specific window arrangement, called a "**Layout**".

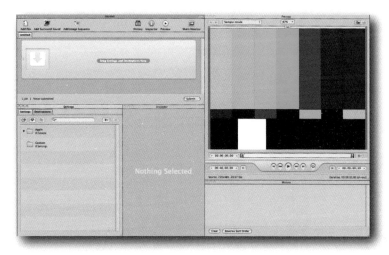

Now let's have a closer look at those 6 core windows. My initial focus will be on each windows behavior and use in the Compressor interface. I will then go into the details of actual functionality.

Windows Menu

❶ The bottom of the Windows Menu lists all the open Batch Windows with a checkbox for the one that has key focus. Please note that a Batch Window is only listed if it is a separate window. If a Batch Window contains 5 Batches as 5 tabs, then only one Batch is listed in the window, the selected Tab.

❷ The middle section of the Window Menu displays all the commands for the other 5 core Windows. Strangely enough all windows have Key Commands assigned to them except the Inspector! Choosing a command will open that window or switch key focus to the window in case it was open already.

❸ A Layout refers to how the 6 core Windows are arranged on the screen. The *Layouts* command opens a menu with 5 default Layouts ❹. However, you can arrange the windows the way you want and save that arrangement as your own Layout. This user Layout will then also be displayed in the Layout list. *Save Layout ...* in the Main Menu and *Save Window Layout...* in the submenu are two different commands that open the same window ❺. It lets you enter your own Layout name. The same naming inconsistency with two differently named commands that mean the same thing is *Manage Layouts...* and *Edit Window Layouts...* Those commands open a window where you can edit the Layout list ❻. When you launch Compressor, it will remember the final window arrangement from the time you quit the app.

The Layouts are stored in *UserName/Library/Application Support/Compressor/Layouts/*. You can move them between computers (while Compressor is not running!)

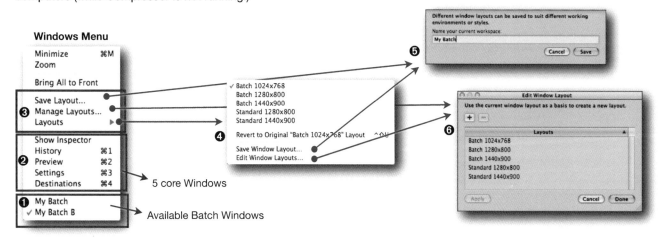

⇒ Batch Window(s)

The Batch Window is the most important window because it represents the "document" of the application. As I mentioned before, this is the only window type that can have multiple windows.

Toolbar

One specialty about the Batch Window is that it has a Toolbar. As with other OS X applications, you can "Customize" the Toolbar to set it up the way you want it. You can also hide the Toolbar all together. Please keep in mind that the commands and user interface elements are slightly different in OS X 10.6 (Snow Leopard) and 10.7 (Lion).

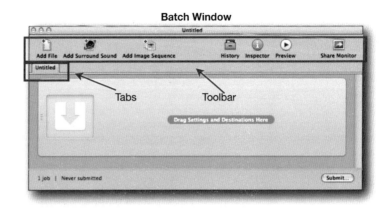

File Menu

Most of the commands in the File Menu belong to the Batch Window.

The *New - Open - Save* commands relate to the Batch as the *document* in the Compressor application.

The *Close Window* command affects any of the 6 core windows that currently has the key focus (indicated by a slightly lighter gray window header).

Please keep in mind that any new Batch you open in Compressor (with the *New* or *Open* command) will not create a new Batch Window. Instead, the new Batch will be added as a new Tab to the active Batch Window.

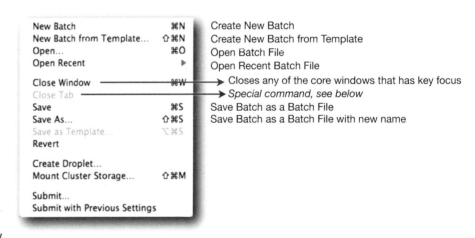

Here is a little subtlety that could go unnoticed.

❶ If the Batch Window has only one tab, then the *Close Tab* command is grayed out and the *Close Window* with the Key Command **cmd+W** will close the window.

❷ If the Batch Window holds more than one tab and one of them has key focus, then the *Close Tab* command is active. This one has now the Key Command **cmd+W** assigned to it! The command *Close Window* now has a different Key Command assignment **sh+cmd+W**.

This might look a little bit confusing unless you think of the Key Command **cmd+W** as *Close Batch*. Then it doesn't matter if it is a standalone window (Close Window) or one of the tabs on a window (Close Tab).

❶   ❷

Tabs

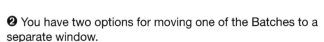

❶ The following screenshots demonstrate how to manage tabs. The example starts with a Batch Window that holds 3 (Batch) tabs: "My Batch A", "My Batch B" and "My Batch C".

❷ You have two options for moving one of the Batches to a separate window.

▸ Right Click Action: **Right-click** on the tab and select the little command window *Tear Off Tab*.

▸ Click-drag Action: **Click-drag** the tab away from the tab header. A little "ghost window" separates from the main window to indicate the separation to a new window.

Right-click action

Click-drag action

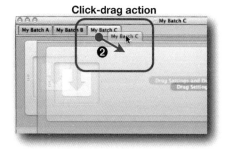

❸ With either action, you now end up with two Batch Windows. One is holding the remaining two Batches "My Batch A" and "My Batch B". The second window holds the now separated "My Batch C".

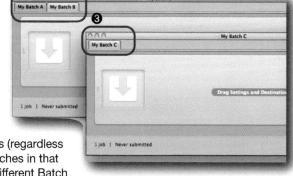

❹ You have the same two action types if you want to move Batches in the opposite direction and move a Batch tab from one Batch Window to a different Batch Window.

▸ Right Click Action: **Right-click** on the tab area of the destination Batch Window. A popup list displays all the currently open Batches (regardless of the window location). The ones with the check mark are the Batches in that window. The ones without a check mark are Batches that are on different Batch Windows. Selecting one of those Batches will move it to the current window.

▸ Click-drag Action: **Click-drag** a tab from any Batch Window onto the tab area of another Batch Window. A little "ghost window" displays the movement. When the tab area of the Destinations Window gets a blue border, release the mouse and the tab will snap to that Destinations Window.

Right-click action

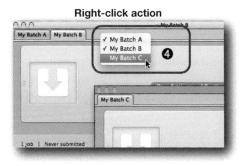

Click-drag action

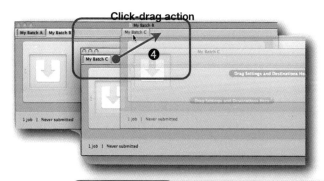

❺ Now you've ended up with only one window again that holds the three Batches, "My Batch A", "My Batch B" and "My Batch C".

Of course you also can re-arrange the tabs on a window by dragging them left or right.

➡ Settings Window

➡ Destinations Window

The relationship between the Settings and Destinations Window is hard to understand. Their GUI behavior doesn't make much sense. It's confusing and possibly buggy.

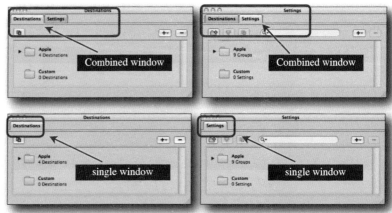

- Using the command to open either the Destinations Window or the Settings Window will open one window that includes two tabs, one for the Settings and one for the Destinations.

- You can use the same "Right Click" or "Click Drag" actions to tear off the tab and have them both displayed as separate windows. Use the same techniques to combine them into one window again.

But now it gets even stranger:

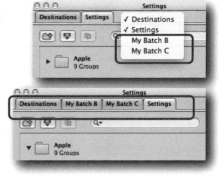

- If the Batch Window, for example, holds several Batch tabs, then those Batches will also be displayed in the tab list of the Settings or Destinations Windows. You can move those Batches to the Settings or Destinations Windows.

- The first tab in the Batch Window however is not available in the list.

- Batches can be moved as tabs to the Settings and Destinations Window but the Settings and Destinations tab can't be moved to a Batch Window. The manual claims that you can do it but I couldn't make it work, neither under Snow Leopard nor Lion.

- After moving tabs around between windows, the list doesn't display all the available Batch tabs. After a restart it's back to normal. Seems like a bug.

- Other core windows (i.e. History) can't be moved to the Settings or Destinations Window at all.

The reason why I'm pointing all this out is so you are aware of it. You can then decide to either not use this inconsistent and buggy part of the interface in the first place, or at least be prepared when you come across it and just ignore it. My guess is that Apple didn't put much effort into cleaning up some of the old code. This is similar to the lack of attention we saw when it came to the overall look of the application.

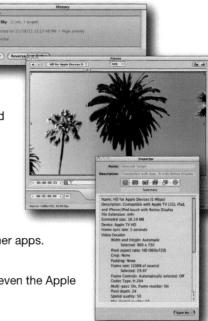

➡ History

This window is a plain application window that can be opened or closed but can't be combined with any other window as a tab.

➡ Viewer

The Viewer window is also a standalone window that is linked to the currently selected Batch.

➡ Inspector

This is the second linked-type window. It displays its content depending on the selection of other windows or elements in those window. It is the only window that can't be re-sized.

The Inspector has two anomalies when compared to typical Inspector Windows in other apps.

- It is not a floating window, meaning, it can be covered by other window.

- This is the only core window that doesn't have a Key Command assigned to it, not even the Apple standard **opt+cmd+I**. Another case of sloppy GUI design, maybe?

➡ All 6 core windows

And finally, let's compare all the 6 core windows again in the context of the window type.

▶ **Document Windows**: In the case of Compressor, these are the Batch Windows.

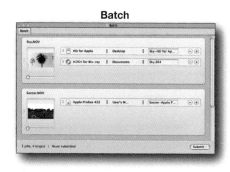

▶ **Application Windows**: The windows that display generic application related information. Settings Window, Destinations Window, History Window.

▶ **Linked Windows**: The special window type that changes their content in relation to other selected windows or elements inside those windows. Batch, Settings and Destinations are the windows that can have their content displayed and edited in the two linked windows: The Preview Window and the Inspector Window.

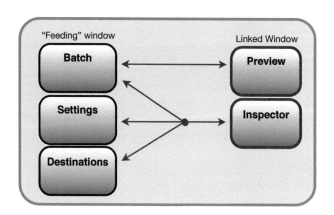

This relationship requires special attention:

- If a Linked Window doesn't have key focus:
  In this case, the Preview and Inspector Window change their displayed data, depending on what Batch, Settings or Destinations Window or window element in them is selected. It is like a read-only situation.

- If a Linked Window has key focus:
  In this case, the Preview or Inspector Window is selected. The question however is, what data are they displaying? It's the data from the one window that was selected right before you selected the Preview or the Inspector. This is the part where you have to pay attention because the data in the Preview and Inspector is not only displayed, you also can edit that data. If you are not sure where it "belongs to", then you can potentially change the wrong settings.

This diagram shows what main windows can "feed" data to the linked Preview and Inspector Window.

Preview:
The Preview is only linked to the selected elements in a Batch Window.

Inspector:
In this case, three windows (Batch, Settings, Destinations) can feed their content to the linked Inspector Window for viewing and editing.

Basic Procedure

Equipped now with the terminology and the interface elements, lets get into the actual functionality of Compressor and how to use it.

Here are the basic steps for a transcoding process in Compressor. As you see, each step contains one term that we discussed earlier in the "Terminology" chapter. Every configuration for a transcoding process in Compressor follows these steps. Be aware that some steps are performed automatically by Compressor. In that case, you can move to the next step.

1. Create a New **Batch**
2. Create a New **Job** (one empty Job is created automatically)
3. Select a **Source Media File** for the Job
4. Create a new **Target** for that Job
5. Assign a **Setting** for that Target
6. Assign a **Destination** for that Target
7. Check/Change the **Name** for the Output Media File in that Target
8. Click **Submit** to start the transcoding
9. (Choose optional Cluster setup)
10. Monitor the process (optional)

Let's look at each step in more detail.

Batch

There are three different options for Step 1:

▶ **Launch Compressor**

You launch the application and a new Batch Window with one Tab will be displayed. This is different than other document-based applications where you just start the blank app without any default document.

▶ **Create a new Batch**

Once the application is running, you can use the Batch that was created during launch and continue the setup or create more additional Batches with those two commands.

- *File > New Batch* or Key Command **cmd+N** to create a new Batch.
- *File > New Batch from Template ...* or Key Command **sh+cmd+N** to create a new Batch with the option to choose a setting from the Template Chooser (explained on the next page).

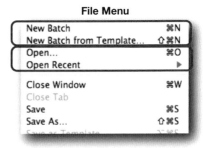

▶ **Open an existing Batch**

The third option is to load an existing Batch that was previously saved as a Batch File.

You have the two standard commands.

- *File > Open ...* or Key Command **cmd+O** to open the file selector window and navigate to a Batch File.
- *File > Open Recent >* to select from the list of previously opened Batch Files.

Template Chooser

This is an optional window that pops up during the creation of a new Batch or when Compressor is launched.

When Compressor creates a new Batch, it creates an empty Job with no Target. Choosing from a set of predefined templates creates a Target for the new Job with the Target Setting defined by that Template. Basically the Templates are "Predefined Targets"

The upper section of the window displays the available Templates. When you select one, its description and Settings name will be displayed in the lower section of the window.

The window has six default Templates, but you can create your own Templates by selecting a Target with a Setting that you want to store as a Template and choose from the Main Menu *File > Save as Template ...* or use the Key Command **opt+cmd+S**. You can enter a name and a description and it will be displayed from now on in the Template Chooser.

Save as Template window

Compressor's Preferences window has three settings that determine the details of how the new Batch is created.

▸ **For New Batches:** The two radio buttons ❶ determine whether or not the Template Chooser is displayed.

▸ **Default Setting**: If you choose not to display the Template Chooser or click Cancel when it pops up, then the new Batch will have an empty Job with no Target (if "None" ❷ is selected) or it will create a Target with the Setting that you choose from that popup menu ❸.

▸ **Default Destination**: If the new Batch creates a Target, then the selection from this popup menu ❹ will be the Destination for the Target.

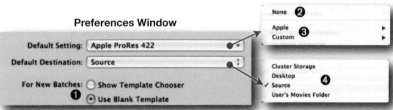

Here is an illustration to show what elements are involved in which actions and their outcome on the newly created Batch:

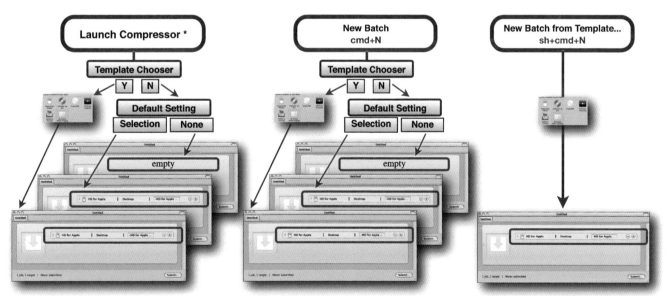

* This procedure for the Launch Compressor is the behavior in OSX 10.5 (Snow Leopard). OSX 10.6 (Lion) has one additional condition:

> When you quit Compressor while a Batch is selected, the next time you launch Compressor, that one Batch will be re-opened after launch (no creating of a new Batch or opening Template Chooser). If you had multiple Batches open in Compressor when you quit, only the one that was selected last will be re-opened during the next launch.

Job

The next step after the Batch is the Job. Remember a Batch can contain one or many Jobs. A newly created Batch will automatically create an empty Job.

Just for demonstration purposes, I deleted that one Job and ended up with an empty Batch in order to start on the lowest level. "Create a Job".

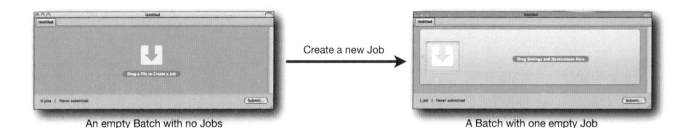

An empty Batch with no Jobs   A Batch with one empty Job

Here are the basic commands related to Jobs:

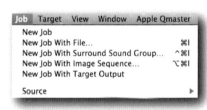

- Create a New Job with any of the following commands:
  - Select a Batch for which you want to create a Job and select one of the 5 Menu Commands in the Job Menu or use their Key Commands.
  - **Right-Click** on the Batch Window and choose from the Contextual Menu.
  - **Drag** a Source Media File onto the Batch Window.
- Delete a Job: Just select it and hit the **delete** key.
- Copy a Job: use the standard copy-paste commands or drag a Job from one Batch Window to another Batch Window. You will see a "ghost" job during the dragging process.

Batch Window: Contextual Menu

Source Media File

As we now know, a Job is defined by one Source Media File and one or many Targets. Now is the time to find out what qualifies as a Source Media File, or in other words, what kind of files can Compressor transcode.

There are four types of Source Media Files:

▶ Any media file. A video, audio or image file.

▶ A Surround Sound audio file.

▶ An Image Sequence. This is a folder that contains a group of numbered image files that make up the sequence.

▶ Target Output. Here you define the output of a Target as the Source for another Job to transcode multiple Jobs in a chain.

There are many ways to select a Source Media File for a Job. You either create a new Job with the Source selection or select a Source for an existing Job.

- Create a new Job with the Source selection:
  - **Drag** a Media File anywhere onto the Batch Window.
  - Select one of the 5 Menu Commands in the Job Menu or use their Key Commands.
  - **Right-Click** on the Batch Window and choose from the Contextual Menu.
- Select a Source for an existing Job (new selection or overwrite existing selection):
  - **Drag** a Media File onto the Source area of the Job.
  - Make a selection from the Main Menu *Jobs > Source >* or use the Key Commands.
  - **Right-click** on the Source area to select from the Contextual Menu.
  - Use the commands in the Toolbar: "*Add Files*", "*Add Surround Sound*", "*Add Image Sequence*".

Source: Contextual Menu

Toolbar

Surround Sound Group

This is a special Media File type for surround sound files intended for transcoding to a surround sound format (i.e. AC3)

A stereo sound file has two channels but they are carried in one single sound file that you can select as the source of a Job for transcoding. Surround Sound mixes on the other hand are usually mixed in discrete channels. That means a 5.1 surround mix ends up with 6 sound files. However you can place only one Source Media File onto a Job. This is what the *Surround Sound Group* is for.

You can use two methods to create a Surround Sound Group:

▶ **Automatic Assignment**

If the discrete audio files of a surround mix have the proper ending (-L, -R, -C, -Ls, -Rs, -S, -LFE), then you can select all those files together in the Finder and drag them onto the Source area of the Job. Compressor will recognize the files and assign them to the correct channels.

▶ **Manual Assignment**

Using this method, you can manually assign any audio file to any channel. Select the Surround Source Group as the Source for a Job and a sheet will slide out under the Batch Window. Here you make the assignment.

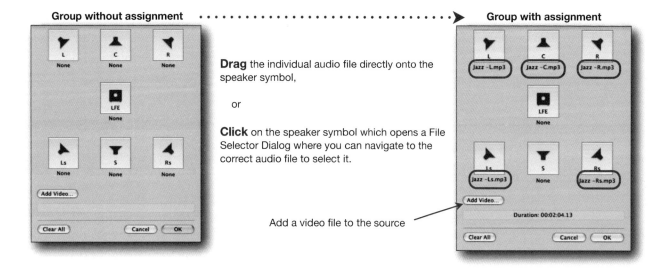

Group without assignment ·····················▶ **Group with assignment**

Drag the individual audio file directly onto the speaker symbol,

or

Click on the speaker symbol which opens a File Selector Dialog where you can navigate to the correct audio file to select it.

Add a video file to the source

In addition to that:

- You don't have to assign all the channels.
- You can add a video file to the Group.
- The total length of the file will be displayed at the bottom.
- Click the "Clear All" button to reset the assignment.

Inspector for Surround Source

Editing Surround Sound Group:

Once you click OK in that window, you can't get back. If you select the Surround Sound Group again from the Source, the un-assigned window will open so you better click Cancel and not OK, otherwise you would erase your current Surround Sound Group.

However you can edit the Group by selecting the Source and opening the Inspector. Under the "A/V Attributes, the same window with the channels assignment will be displayed and this one you can edit.

Image Sequence

Similar to the Surround Sound Group where you select a group of audio files as the Job Source, the Image Sequence lets you select a group of image files as a Job Source.

- Select "Image Sequence" as the source which opens a File Selector Dialog. Navigate to the folder (not the files) that contain the images and select it.

Editing Image Sequence:

The editing and final setup for the Image Sequence has to be done again in the Inspector under the
A/V Attributes tab:

- The "i" button opens a window which displays all the images in that sequence. You cannot add files to this window.
- The Native Field Dominance popup menu lets you select from "*Progressive*", "*Top first*" and "*Bottom first*".
- The Frame rate popup menu provides a list of common frame rates.
- You can even assign an audio file to the image sequence.
- The rest of the Inspector tab displays various attributes.

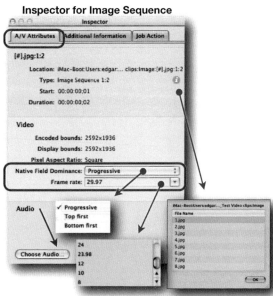

Inspector for Image Sequence

Target Output

With this selection, you choose a Source Media File that doesn't exist yet. The Source will be the Output Media File of a Target from another Job, creating a transcoding chain. "Take file **A** and transcode it with the setting **x** and then take that transcoded file Ax and use it to apply transcoding **y**, creating the final Output file "**Axy**"

Here is the procedure:

- Create a Job, do the usual setup, and select the Target (or multiple Targets)
- Select the command from the Main Menu *Job > New Job with Target Output* or the Target Contextual Menu
- A new linked Job is created with the chain link logo. The Source name is the same as the Output Media File name of the Source Job
- Select a new Target for that linked Job and continue with the transcoding setup.
- (optional) You could daisy chain even more Jobs.
- When you Submit the Batch, each Job is transcoded and then fed into the next Job for the next transcoding. Each Output Media file from each step is available at the end of the transcoding process.

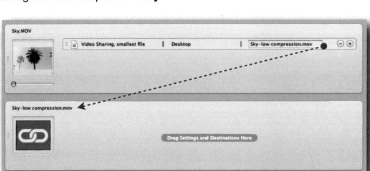

➡ Other Source related stuff:

- The Source thumbnail provides a slider ❶ that lets you skim through the video (if the media file contains video or images)
- There are two Contextual Menus that carry the Source commands and the "Clear Source" command when you **right-click** on the Source area ❷ or **right-click** on the Job area ❸
- You can drag the Source thumbnail between Jobs or use the cut-copy-paste commands from the Contextual Menus

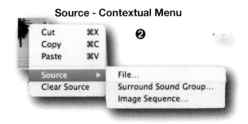

Source - Contextual Menu

Job - Contextual Menu

Target

Once you have the Job created and the Source for it selected, you go to the next step and create the Target for the Job.

There are two commands available from the Main Menu and also from the Job's Contextual Menu:

> ▶ *Target > New Target:* This creates an empty Target.

> ▶ *Target > New Target With Setting...* : This creates a Target with specific settings. Once selected, a sheet slides out under the Batch Window that lets you select the Setting. (This is the same content as displayed in the Settings Window). The Contextual Menu provides a submenu from where you can navigate to the specific Setting.

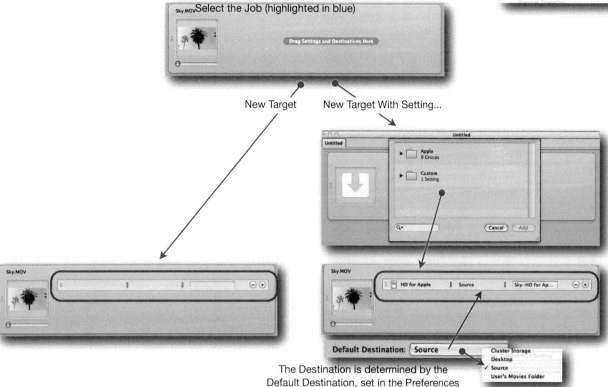

The Destination is determined by the Default Destination, set in the Preferences

> ▶ There is another command for adding a Target to a Job. If at least one Target is assigned to the Job, you can use the "plus" button on that Target to add another empty Target to the Job

add new Target

remove Target

> ▶ You can also drag a Setting from the Settings Window or a Destination from the Destinations Window onto a Job or the Batch Window to create a new Target with only that Setting or only that Destination assigned to it.

➡ Manage Targets:

• Delete Targets:

  • Select one or more Targets and hit the **delete** key or **cmd+X.**

  • Click the minus button at the right end of the Target.

• Move Targets between Jobs: **drag** the Target to a new Job, even onto a different Batch Window.

• Copy Targets to a new or the same Job: select the Target, hit **cmd+C**, select the destination Job and hit **cmd+V** or use the copy-paste commands from the Target's Contextual Menu.

Settings

On to the next Step, the Settings. These are the instructions for the transcoding process that can be assigned to a Target in different ways:

▸ Select a Target and use the command *"Change Setting..."*, available from:

  • Main Menu *Target > Change Setting...*

  • **Right-click** on the Target to select the command from the Contextual Menu.

Both commands open the same Settings sheet that slides out under the Batch Window to select a Setting. The content is identical to the Settings Window (details about the Settings Window below).

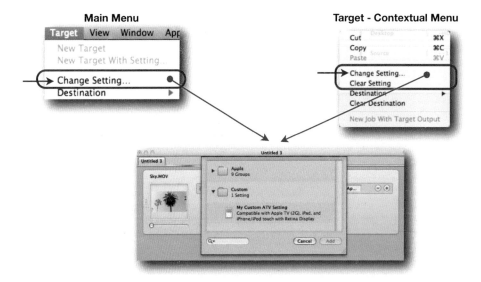

▸ You can also drag a Setting directly from the Settings Window onto the Target.

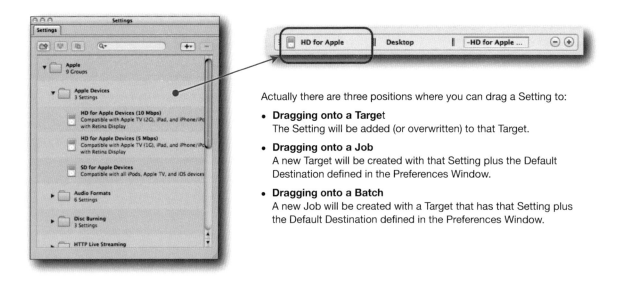

Actually there are three positions where you can drag a Setting to:

• **Dragging onto a Target**
  The Setting will be added (or overwritten) to that Target.

• **Dragging onto a Job**
  A new Target will be created with that Setting plus the Default Destination defined in the Preferences Window.

• **Dragging onto a Batch**
  A new Job will be created with a Target that has that Setting plus the Default Destination defined in the Preferences Window.

➡ Manage Settings:

• Delete Setting: select "Clear Setting" from the Contextual Menu.

• Copy Setting: dragging a Target over an existing Target will copy only the Setting, overwriting the existing Setting. The Destination will not be overwritten. The Name will be overwritten unless it was given a custom name before.

Destination

The Destination, the location where the Output Media File will be saved to, can be assigned to a Target in different ways:

▸ Select a Target and use the command "Destination...", available from:
   - Main Menu *Target > Destination >*
   - **Right-click** on the Target to select the command from the Contextual Menu.

The command opens a submenu which lists all the Destinations that are defined in the Destinations Window (details about the Destinations Window below).

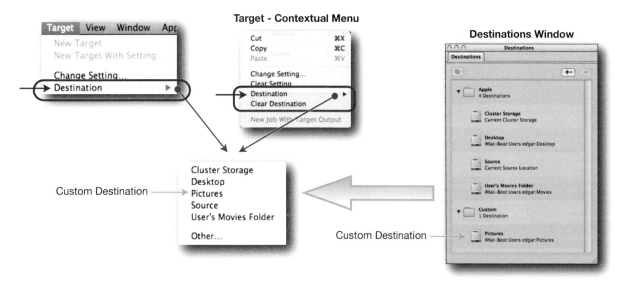

▸ You can also drag a Destination directly from the Destinations Window onto the Target.

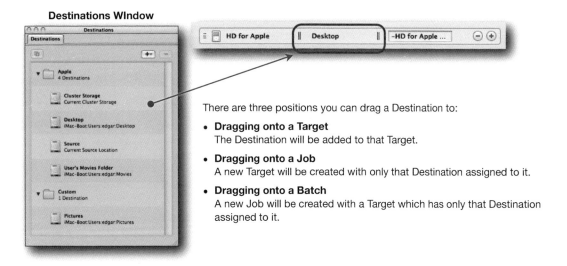

There are three positions you can drag a Destination to:

- **Dragging onto a Target**
  The Destination will be added to that Target.

- **Dragging onto a Job**
  A new Target will be created with only that Destination assigned to it.

- **Dragging onto a Batch**
  A new Job will be created with a Target which has only that Destination assigned to it.

- **Cluster Storag**e: see chapter about rendering.
- **Other...** : opens a File Selector Dialog where you can select any location on the drive.

➡ Manage Settings:

- Delete Destination: select "Clear Destination" from the Contextual Menu.
- You cannot move or copy a Destination by itself between Targets or Jobs.
- You can set a Default Destination in the Preferences window. That Destination is used when a new Target is created.

Name

The third section of a Target is the filename that the Output Media File will get after transcoding.

Name for the Output Media File

▶ Automatic file naming:

As a default, the name will be automatically created based on the "Output Filename Template" which is stored with each Destination. Templates are "instructions" on how to create the file name. On the right is an example of a Template (see next chapter for details).

The Name will be dynamically updated when changing the Source file, the Setting or the Destination.

Example: Source filename "**Sky**", Setting name "**HD for Apple**"   Output Media filename: **Sky - HD for Apple.m4a**

▶ Manual file naming:

You can overwrite the automatic filename at any time. Once you've named it manually, it will no longer be updated dynamically when you change the Source file or Setting.

If the font color of the filename turns red and has a yellow warning sign, then it means that the name exists already in that location (most likely after a successful transcoding process).

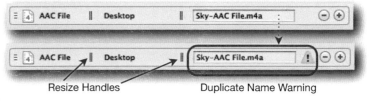

Resize Handles   Duplicate Name Warning

Please note: You can resize the space for the three Target sections by dragging the vertical handles

Submit

Batch Status

Each Batch Window displays the Batch Status at the bottom of the window where you can see how many Jobs and Targets are contained in this Batch. It also lists if and when the Batch was submitted.

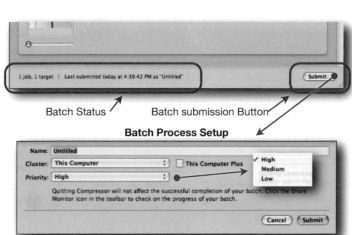

Batch Status   Batch submission Button

Batch Submission Button

The Submit button slides out a sheet where you can setup the Batch Process.

- Name: Gives the Batch Process a name to identify it better when monitoring multiple batch processes later.

- Cluster: This determines who is doing the processing. Leave it at the default setting "Computer". For Cluster details, see the chapter about Rendering.

- Priority: You can set different priorities when sending more Batches for processing.

Clicking the Submit Button will start the process. Please note that the process is handed over to an application in the background and is not preformed by Compressor. Closing Compressor doesn't affect the ongoing transcoding process.

Monitor

I will discuss this topic in the separate chapter below.

Preview

Now that you have an understanding of the basic procedures in Compressor, let's move on to the Preview Window. It doesn't look too complicated, maybe similar to the Viewer in FCPx. However, the few selections you can make in this window, have consequences that you must understand in order to use it properly. Additionally, it is a linked window. That means, it is important to know what content from the Batch Window is feeding into the Preview Window. So instead of just going through the various elements of the window, I want to wheel back a bit.

Here's a quick flashback first. The basic diagram that shows what Compressor is doing, has three elements. You give Compressor a Source Media File and tell it to transcode the file to a new Output Media File based on instructions (Settings) that you define.

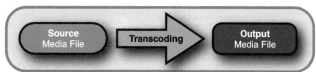

Now the main question is, what does the Output Media File look like after the transcoding. You can play your Source file in its original state, but in order to find out if the instructions for the transcoding were correct, you have to process them in Compressor first. After that, you can play the Output Media File and see if it turned out the way you "envisioned it". This however is not very practical because the actual transcoding process could take from a couple of minutes up to a couple of hours depending on the length of the source file and the complexity of the transcoding (besides processing power).

That's were the Preview Window comes in. Compressor has the ability to simulate the transcoding process in real time so you can pre-view it before committing to the transcoding settings and the process. It simulates the Output Media File ❸.

The Preview Window can display two signals: the Input of the Transcoding module ❶ which is identical to the Source Media File, and the Output of the Transcoding module ❷ which is the output of the Settings section.

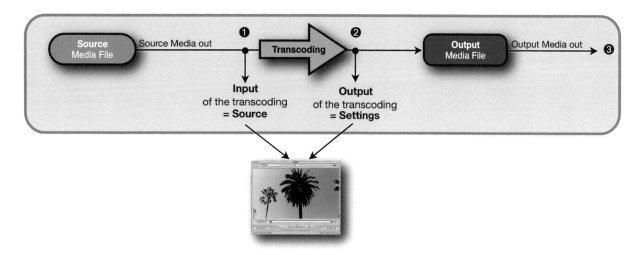

As you can see, different terms could mean the same thing. Compressor is not consistent at using the same terminology, so you have to be flexible and know those identical terms when looking at the Preview Window.

Batch Item

So where are the controls in the Preview Window that let you choose what is displayed on the screen?

This is where our previously learned understanding of linked windows comes into play. Remember, the Preview is a linked window. Its displayed content depends on the selection of another window, the Batch Window. Please note that it is not only the matter what Batch Window is selected, but what specific element in that Batch Window is selected. That selection is called a **Batch Item**.

> A **Batch Item** can be either a **Job** or a **Target**

And here again are different terms for the same thing.

A Batch Window can have three states regarding what Batch Item is selected:

- ▶ **Nothing** is selected. Nothing in the Batch Window is selected.
- ▶ A **Job** is selected. This is the same as:
    - A **Source** is selected. Because each Job can have only one Source Media File assigned to it.
    - The **Input** is selected: The Source Media File is the Input of the the Target.
- ▶ A **Target** is selected. This is same as:
    - A **Setting** is selected: Each Target has one transcoding Setting.
    - An **Output** is selected: This refers to the output of the Settings module or the "Simulated Output" as a simulation of the final Output Media File (another used term is *Destination*).

(In the context of the Preview, we ignore the fact for now that you could select multiple Jobs or multiple Targets)

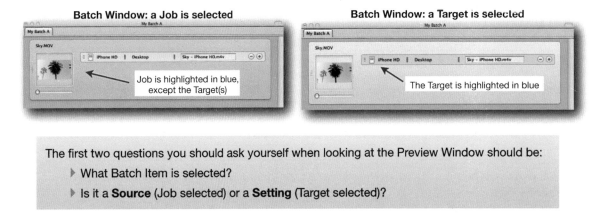

The first two questions you should ask yourself when looking at the Preview Window should be:
- ▶ What Batch Item is selected?
- ▶ Is it a **Source** (Job selected) or a **Setting** (Target selected)?

❶ The **Batch Item popup menu** displays all the Jobs (Sources) and their Targets (Settings) of the currently selected Batch Window. You can make a different selection in the Batch Window, and the popup menu changes the selection accordingly. The link also works the other way around. Selecting a different item from the popup menu in the Preview Window will make that selection in the linked Batch Window active.

❷ The **Batch Item selection buttons** let you step through the popup menu, selecting the next or previous item.

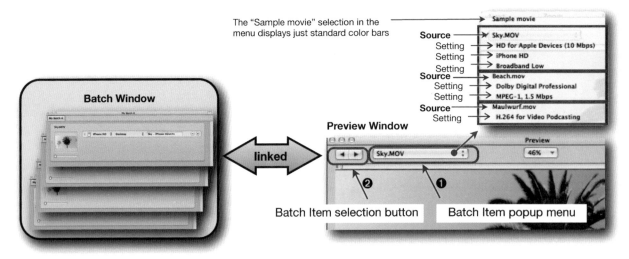

So the selected Batch Item can be either a Source or a Setting. Now the question is, what will be displayed in the Preview:

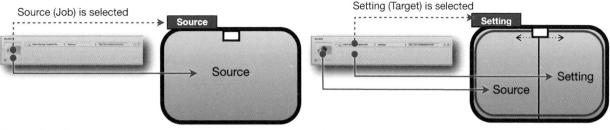

Source (Input)
If a the selected Batch item is a Source (Job), then the Preview Frame will display the content of the Source Media File (Input)

Setting (Output)
If a the selected Batch item is a Setting (Target) then the Preview Display functions as a split screen with a vertical divider. The left side displays the portion of the Source Media File (Input) and the right side displays the output of the Settings module (Output). In addition, you will see red Cropping Boundaries. (discussed later).

What am I looking at ?

The split screen slider at the top of the screen lets you slide the vertical divider line to the left or right. Remember, you always look at one frame, and by moving the divider line, you decide how much of the portion you want to see from the Input (Source) or from the Output (Setting). When moving the slider all the way to the right you would view only the Source signal, when moving the slider all the way to the left, you would view only the Setting signal.
You can even move the slider during playback.

When looking at the Preview Window, these are the three spots to check to know what video you are viewing:
  ▶ Selected Batch Item: name of a Source file or name of a Setting.
  ▶ Split Screen Slider: with or without the white divider line.
  ▶ Red Cropping Boundaries: visible or not.

When you have some settings applied (color adjustments, text overlay, etc), it is easier to see the"left/right" or "before/after" effect and know that a Setting is selected.

Helper Tag:

The yellow helper tags (also known as tool tips) are a standard GUI feature that are used in virtually all applications. When you move the mouse over an object (menu, controller, etc) a yellow tag will appear for a few seconds with a short description of that object. The description for the objects we just discussed is a further indication that the Compressor app is a little bit "unorganized", because it uses different terminology in the helper tags than in the manual.

Batch Item selection: Choose input/output to view   Split Screen Slider: Adjust the Source and Destination split

Frame Size

Before I discuss the next element of the Preview Window, I want to take another detour to discuss some video terminology.

In the past, the technical side of dealing with video (editing) and with music (recording, mixing) required highly skilled personnel. Handling of film, understanding video technology, microphone technique and mixing, all had foundations in electronics, optics and acoustics, They weren't easy jobs to say the least! But things have changed. Technologies got easier, equipment got cheaper and nowadays everybody can make a movie or record a song with easy to use tools. However, in some areas, there are still "left overs" from the old days. Terminologies have survived that either don't make much sense in the digital age and in some cases can cause confusion if the necessary background is missing.

In the case of video technology, there are many tricky areas caused by the historic transition from black/white to color TV, regional differences of conflicting standards and finally the transition from analog to digital. I want look briefly at the following terms:

Aspect Ratio - Resolution - Frame Size - Video Format - Dimensions

Short explanation, they are basically all the same, describing a Video Frame. Of course, a video is a series of images that is determined by its "speed", how fast the individual frames pass by (Frame Rate). But for now I'm picking only one frame and I'm interested in what parameters describe that frame. Not the content, just the dimensions. And that is what all those terms above have in common. They describe the dimensions of a video frame, which is just a 2-dimensional image when only looking at a single frame.

Frame Size:

This is the easiest term. You can describe the size of a frame by its Width and its Height. The unit will be "pixels". Technically, the pixel is not just a unit but a two dimensional object itself. But that's a whole different kind of manual, so I'll ignore it for now.

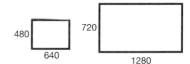

Aspect Ratio:

This is a relative description of the relation between the Width and the Height in the form of a fraction or division.

W:H = 640:480 = 4:3 = 1.333 or W:H = 1280:720 = 16:9 = 1.77

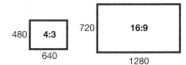

Resolution

When we draw vertical and horizontal lines in a frame at each pixel unit, we end up having a grid with i.e. 1280 vertical lines and 720 horizontal lines. The number of cells in that grid is equal to the product of 1280x720. Although the resolution is a value of how many cells are in a frame ("how fine or how high is the resolution"), the actual product (i.e. 921,600) is not used. Instead, the multiplication expression 1280x720 is used as the resolution because it also carries the information of the width and the hight of the frame and therefore its Aspect Ratio. The number 921,600 tells you how many cells are in a frame but not its aspect Ratio.

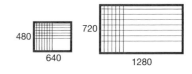

Video Format

This is a term that can describe a whole set of parameters like NTSC, PAL, 720p, 1080i. These are all different Video Formats with their own complex set of description and standards. The Frame Size (and therefore Aspect Ratio) is mostly part of it. For example a Video Format in 720p has a frame size of 1280x720 with the Aspect Ratio of 16:9.

This was a very simplified explanation of those terms, but enough to hopefully avoid confusion for the next few pages. Lets's choose the term **Frame Size** as a representation of the other three terms and ask the question related to Compressor. What do we have to be aware of when we change the Frame Size as part of our transcoding settings?

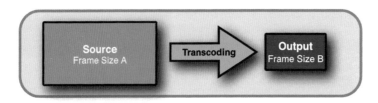

➡ Change Frame Size

What happens when we change the Frame Size of a video to a different Frame Size.

- **Same Aspect Ratio**: If the Aspect Ratio stays the same, then the picture frame is just smaller or bigger (Example B, C)
- **Different Aspect Ratio**: If the Aspect Ratio changes, then you end up with a distorted picture. I looks either squeezed or stretched. (Example D, E)

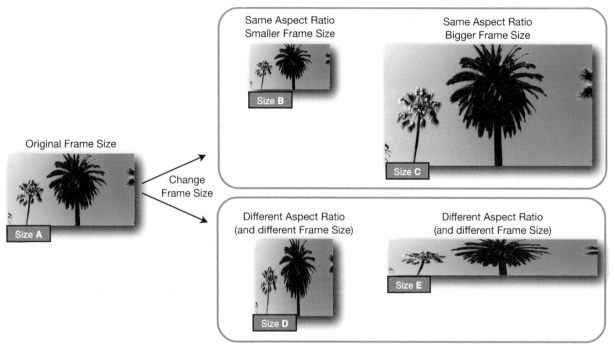

➡ Select a portion of the Frame

With this procedure, you select a portion of the picture and "cut it out", also known as **cropping**. You draw a new frame that has its own Frame Size (Width x Height) and its resulting Aspect Ratio. The cropped Frame Size is smaller than the original Frame Size. You can **scale** it up to have the same Frame Size as the original Frame. Of course, if the Aspect Ratio of the cropped frame is different than the original Aspect Ratio, you also end up with a distorted picture. The "Cropped and Scaled" picture can now be changed to any other Frame Size as in the example above (B, C, D, E).

Preview

27

As we will see later on, we have a lot of parameters and attributes available in the Settings section that let us change the Source Media file. The Frame Size is just one of those. However, here is the reason why the Frame Size is special and why I spent the extra time to explain some fundamentals:

The Preview Window has one frame. It can display the Source and Setting in a special split screen mode. If we change for example the color in the Settings, then the right portion (Setting) would have a different color than the left portion (Source) of the split screen. Not a problem. However, if you choose a different Frame Size in the Setting, then you have a problem. The Preview Window has only one frame and the question is what Frame Size does it use to display the split screen, the Frame Size of the Source or the Frame Size of the Setting. The answer is: You can choose.

 The Preview Window has two buttons in the upper right corner. The manual calls it the "Source/Setting selection" and those button relate to a little display in the lower left corner called "Source/Output information". One of those little inconsistencies.

Here is how it works:

The **Batch Item Selection** (blue) determines what is displayed in the video frame of the Preview.

- Source is selected: The Source Media file will be displayed.
- Setting is selected: The split screen will be displayed with Source and Setting.

The Frame Size Selection (brown) determines what Frame Size is used to display the video:

- Source is selected (left button): The Frame Size of the Source will be used for the Display.
- Setting is selected (right button): The Frame Size of the Setting will be used for the Display.

The Frame Size Display (brown) shows the Frame Size and its selection:

- Source: indicates that the Frame Size of the Source is used.
- Output: indicates that the Frame Size of the Setting (the parameters for the "Output" file) is used.

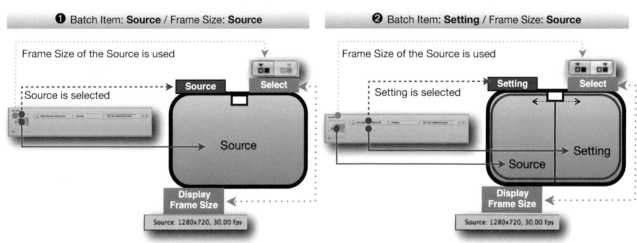

❶ If the selected Batch item is a Source, then the Frame Size Selection can't be switched (grayed out). It can only display the video in the Frame Size of the Source.

❷ Both, Source and Setting video in the split screen are displayed with the Frame Size of the Source. The left portion of the split screen that represents the Source video has the correct Frame Size. The right portion of the split screen that represents the Setting video would display incorrectly (distorted dimensions) if it has a different Frame Size setting than the Source.

❸ Both, Source and Setting video in the split screen are displayed with the Frame Size of the Setting. The right portion of the split screen that represents the Setting video has the correct Frame Size. The left portion of the split screen that represents the Source video would display incorrectly (distorted dimensions) if it has a different Frame Size setting than the Setting.

You can toggle the two buttons for the Frame Size Selection and read the Frame Size Display in the lower left corner to quickly check the Frame Size of the Source and Setting.

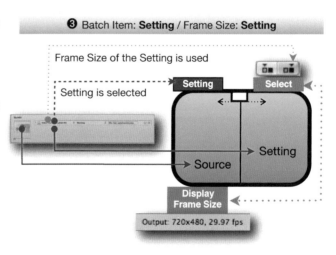

➡ Cropping

Now how does the Cropping feature fit into the whole Batch item and Frame Size selection? Here is a step by step example:

❶ This is the first step where you select a Source to be displayed in the Preview. It displays the correct Frame Size of the Source because that is the only option.

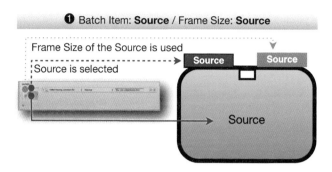

❷ Now you select the Setting from the Batch Item selection. This is the Setting that you're about to configure for the transcoding. Two things happened:

• The display changed to the split screen.
• The red cropping boundaries are displayed.

Please note that the Frame Size selection is still set to Source. As we just discussed, this could mean an incorrect viewing of the Setting video on the right portion of the split screen if it has a different Frame Size configuration in its Setting.

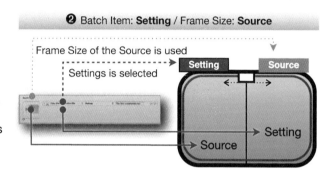

❸ You can use the crop handles on the red cropping boundaries to re-size a cropped frame. Remember, even with the split screen divider, you are looking at one frame. That means that the position of the divider has no affect on the cropping. The important thing is that the cropping dimensions are applied to the current Frame Size selection, which is set to the Frame Size of the Source!

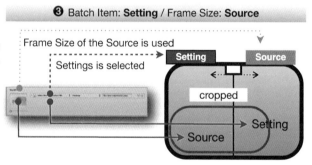

❹ Here is the most important step you have to be aware of. If you made a crop selection and switched the Frame Size selector to display the Setting's Frame Size, two things will happen:

• The crop selection (made in the previous step) is scaled up to the Frame Size of the Setting.
• The crop boundaries disappear

You can toggle the Frame Size selector button between Source and Setting to go back and adjust the crop selection and then check its result again by switching to the Frame Size of the Setting again

Remember, if the Frame Size of the Source is different than the Setting that is displayed, then the Source is not displayed correctly. But that doesn't matter because we are interested in how the Setting (the potential Output Media file) look.

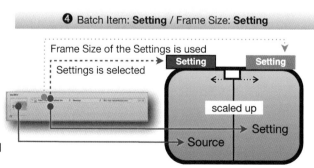

GUI

Now we are done with the "heavy lifting". Once you've digested the basic mechanics regarding the Preview Window, the rest is pretty simple.

The Preview Window provides two functions:

❶ **View**: Realtime preview of the video, before/after transcoding

Playback the video and watch it in real time to see how it will look after the transcoding. This way you can assign and tweak the Setting with visual feedback before committing to them.

❷ **Edit**: Additional Editing

Although all the Transcoding configurations are done in the Inspector, there are a few settings that can be applied directly in the Preview Window: Durations, Markers and Cropping.

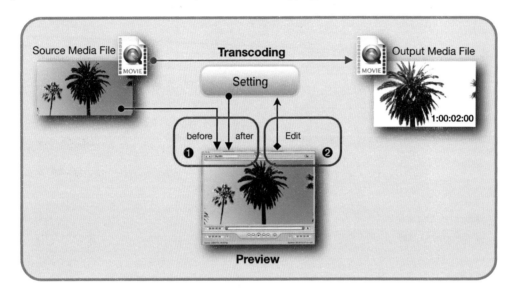

Limitations:

From the four main Components that make up the transcoding Setting, only the *Filter* and *Geometry* settings can be fully previewed. The effect of the *Encoder* and *Frame Control* can only be checked when playing back the Output file after the transcoding process. The exception is the Frame Size which is part of the Encoder settings. As we've just seen, it's settings can be previewed.

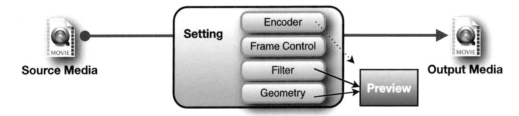

Finally let's go through the list of all the elements and controls in the Preview Window divided into two groups based on the two basic functions: **View** - **Edit**

▸ **Batch Item Popup Menu**: It lists the content of the selected Batch Window and is a representation of all the Jobs and their Targets in that Batch Window. The name of the Source Media file for a Job is listed first, followed by the name(s) of the Setting for each Target. As a linked window, changing the item on the list changes the selection in that Batch Window and vice versa.

▸ **Batch Item Selection Button**: These are "step-through-the-list" buttons. Clicking the left or right arrow button will go up or down the list of the Batch Item Popup Menu.

▸ **Preview Scale Selection:** This scales the Preview Window size to the video frame size. You can choose any of the three values (100%, 75%, 50%) or resize the Preview Window and the video frame will resize accordingly, displaying the resulting % scale. The additional item "Correct for Pixel Aspect Ratio" is for compensation of the various Pixel Aspect Ratios. The Preview Scale settings have no affect on the actual Output Media File. Move the mouse over the menu button to reveal a helper tag that displays the currently displayed Frame Size in Width and Height.

▸ **Frame Size View Selection:** Select which Frame Size is applied to the displayed video. The Frame Size of the Source (left button) or the Frame Size of the Setting (right button). If the Batch Item selection is a Source, then the right button is grayed out.

▸ **Split Screen Slide:** This has only an affect when a Setting is selected from the Batch Item list. Now you can move the split handle left or right. The left portion displays the Source video and the right portion displays the "Setting" video (the video with the transcoding setting applied to it), simulating the to be transcoded Output Media file. You can even move the slider during playback to watch the "before-after" results.

▸ **Timeline with Playhead**: The timeline bar represents the length of the whole video with the yellow Playhead marking the position of the current frame. Its position is displayed in the SMPTE reader to the left of the timeline. You can position the Playhead by clicking on the Timeline or by changing the SMPTE address. The video starts at 0:00:00:00 unless the Source video has its own timecode track embedded.

▸ **Frame Size, Frame Rate**: Displays the current Frame Size and Frame Rate based on the "Frame Size View Selection" buttons.

▸ **Transport Controls**: Typical Transport Controls that are also available as Key Commands: **space** for play/pause, **J** for play backwards 2x, **K** for play forward 2x. **Left arrow** and **right arrow** moves the Playhead by 1 frame.

▸ **Duration**: This displays the duration between the In and Out point.

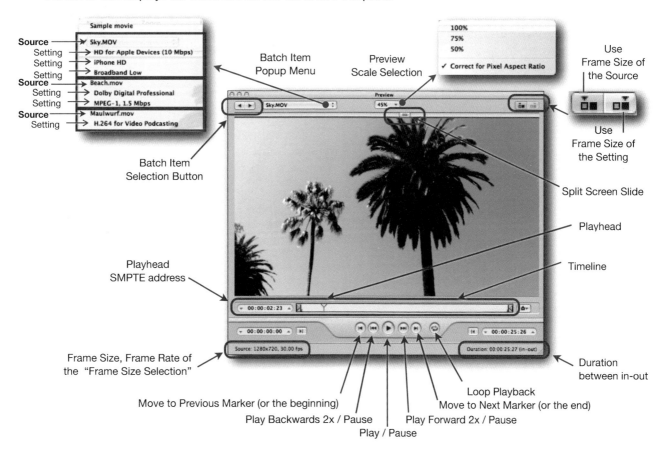

➡ **Edit Elements**

Here are the three parameters of the Transcoding Settings that you can change in the Preview Window:

▶ **In - Out**

This feature is an easy one and also very practical. It is even more important, now that FCPx only allows you to export the full Project and not a section of it (as of version 10.0.2). Instead, you "hand over" a Project to Compressor and set the in and out point there if you want to export only a section of the Project. The selection will be applied to all Targets in that Job during the transcoding.

You can set the In and Out point in different ways:

- Set the playhead to that position and hit the Key Command **I** or **O**
- Move the playhead to a position and click the "Set In point" or "Set Out point" button.
- Adjust the In point SMPTE address or Out point SMPTE address. Use the little up and down arrows, drag the number values up and down or double click on the display and enter a timecode address.
- Slide the In point or Out point Marker on the Timeline.

▶ **Crop**

The red Crop guides are only visible when a Setting (not a Source) is selected in the Batch Item popup menu and the Frame Size View Selection button is set to Source (left button).

- Resize with Crop Handles: You can drag any of the corner or side handles to adjust the crop selection. (Holding down the shift or shift+command key have some aspect ratio restriction when dragging the corner handles)
- Move: You can move the whole crop selection by dragging the selection while keeping its dimensions.
- A display will pop up while dragging. It shows the offset to the left, right, top and bottom between the full frame (Source) and the cropped frame (Output). Those Crop numbers correspond to the Geometry settings in the Inspector.

Again, two selections have to be made for the crop guides to be displayed:

- Select a Setting (not a Source) from the Batch Item popup menu that you want to edit.
- Select the Frame Size of the Source by clicking the left button.

Select the Frame Size of the Setting (right button) to view the result: The cropped selection will be scaled up to the Frame Size of the Setting (the red cropping guide will disappear).

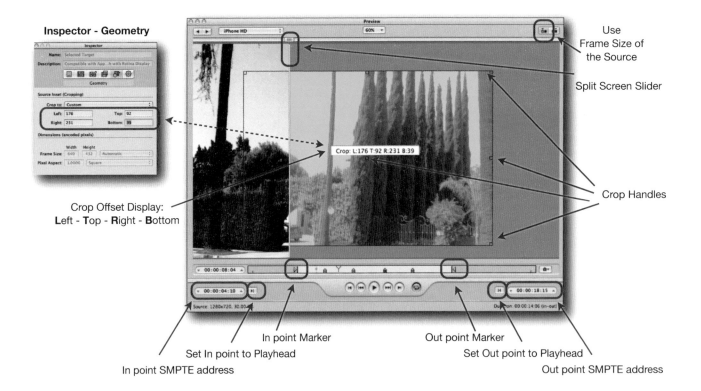

Inspector - Geometry

Use Frame Size of the Source

Split Screen Slider

Crop Handles

Crop Offset Display:
Left - **T**op - **R**ight - **B**ottom

In point Marker · Out point Marker

Set In point to Playhead · Set Out point to Playhead

In point SMPTE address · Out point SMPTE address

▶ **Marker**

Another restriction in the new FCPx are the Markers. Chapter Markers now have to be created in Compressor. Only the following file formats support Markers: MPEG-1, MPEG-2 (Podcast only), QuickTime Movies and H.264 for Apple Devices.

You manage Markers in three areas:

- On the Timeline
- With the transport controls: Go to previous/next Marker
- From the Markers popup menu

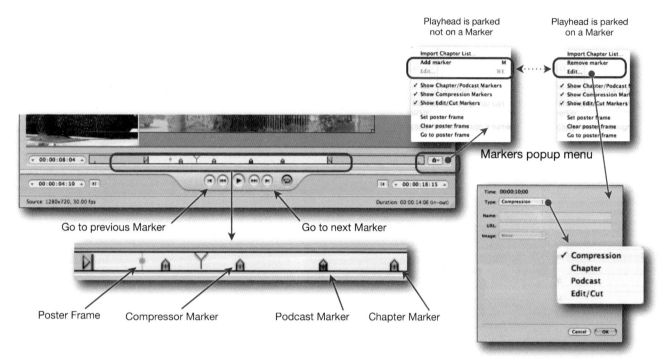

There are four types of Markers plus the Poster Frame:

🎭 Blue - **Compressor Markers**: These are the default markers that you set in Compressor with the Key Command **M**.

🎭 Purple - **Chapter Markers**: Used for DVD and Blu-Ray authoring. You can assign a name, a URL and an image to the marker.

🎭 Red - **Podcast Markers**: Used for Potcasts. You can assign a name, a URL and an image to the marker.

🎭 Green - **Edit/Cut Markers**: These are set automatically at every cut of the imported FCPx sequence. These are special purpose markers also knows an *automatic compression markers.* Compressor uses those markers to improve the compression quality during transcoding by generating MPEG I-frames.

🎭 Gray - **Poster Frame**: This is a special Marker. It marks the frame that is used as a reference image to represent the video file in iTunes or other apps that support that feature. Unlike any of the other Markers, you can have only one Poster Frame.
The Poster Frame, being not really a Marker, has its own three commands in the popup menu:
Set Poster Frame, *Clear Poster Frame*, *Goto Poster Frame*

The Markers popup menu lets you choose which type of markers to display on the timeline.

- Show Chapter/Podcast Markers
- Show Compression Markers
- Show Edit/Cut Markers

Import Chapter List

This is a special command that lets you import a plain text file that contains a Markers list. The format is fairly simple. One line per Marker and each line has two entries: The timecode address (hh:mm:ss:ff) and the name of the Marker. Both entries can be separated by comma, space or tab. The Markers don't have to be in chronological order and any line that doesn't start with the timecode will be ignored (useful for comments). The imported Markers will be Chapter Markers.

Here is how to manage Marker:

💡 Add a Marker

This is a two step process: First, place the Playhead on the timeline where you want to create the Marker and then create the Marker with one of the following commands:

- Use the Key Command **M** (the command toggles the Marker set/remove).
- Use the *Add Marker* command from the Marker popup menu. The command changes to *Remove Marker* when the Playhead is parked on a Marker.

💡 Delete a Marker

Again a two step process: First, place the Playhead on the Marker that you want to delete by using the transport control button "Goto Previous/Next Marker" and then choose one of the two commands:

- Use the Key Command **M** (the command toggles the Marker create/remove).
- Use the *Remove Marker* command from the Marker popup menu. This command is only visible in the popup menu when the Playhead is parked exactly on a Marker.

💡 Edit a Marker

Another two step process: First, place the Playhead on the Marker that you want to edit by using the transport control button "Goto Previous/Next Marker" and then choose one of the two commands:

- Use the Key Command **cmd+E**
- Use the *Edit...* command from the Marker popup menu.

The Edit command opens a separate Edit sheet. The Edit sheet is slightly different depending on the to be edited Marker.

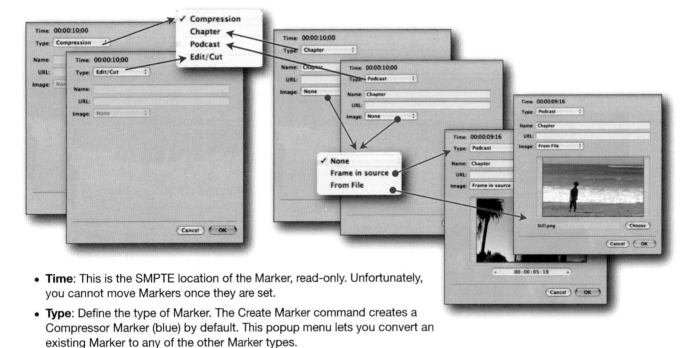

- **Time**: This is the SMPTE location of the Marker, read-only. Unfortunately, you cannot move Markers once they are set.
- **Type**: Define the type of Marker. The Create Marker command creates a Compressor Marker (blue) by default. This popup menu lets you convert an existing Marker to any of the other Marker types.
- **Name**: Give the Marker a name. This will only be visible in the Output file on supported file formats (Chapter Marker and Podcast Marker only).
- **URL**: This will be the active link for a Marker Image that will only be visible in the Output file for Podcast Markers.
- **Image**: Assign an image to a Chapter Marker or Podcast Marker. A popup menu lets you choose either a frame from the current video (*Frame in source*) or import any image file from your hard drive (*From File*).

Destinations

Before going through the individual parameters and functionality of the Destinations, let's look first at the diagram below, that shows the Destination in the big picture.

On top, we see the familiar three elements: **Source Media File - Transcoding - Output Media File**. But before we can click the Submit button and start the process, we have to tell Compressor two more things:

▶ Where should the Output Media File be stored? At what location?

▶ What should be the Name for the Output Media File?

Usually, this kind of decision is made after a *Save* command that opens a File Selector Dialog. There you enter a file name and navigate to the location where you want to save the file. In the case of Compressor, this is not very practical, because here you can setup multiple transcoding processes and transcode them all at once, in one "Batch".

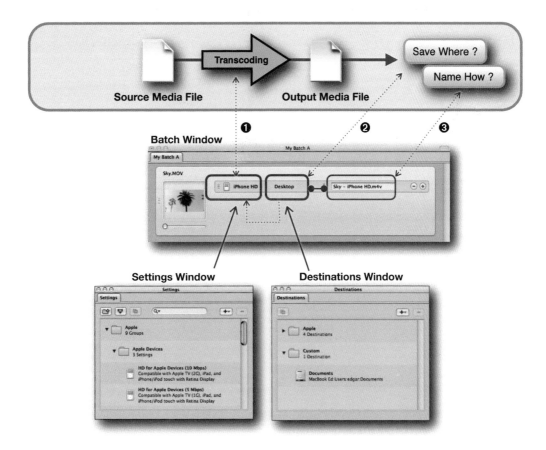

As we've seen earlier, the configuration of a Transcoding process (Target) contains three elements:

❶ **Setting**: This includes the parameters that determine the transcoding process. The Settings Window contains all the available configurations to choose from.

❷ **Destination**: The Destinations Window contains all the preconfigured Destinations to choose from.

❸ **File Name**: Each Destination lets you also define a rule that automatically creates the File Name in a specific way (explained below). The file name is automatically created in the Target in an entry box based on those rules. The name can be overwritten manually.

Target

Managing Destinations

The Destinations are managed in the Destinations Window. The window only contains:

▶ Three controls: **Duplicate**, **Add**, **Remove** a Destination.

▶ Two folders:

- **Apple**: this folder contains four default Destinations that can't be changed or removed.
  - *Source*: The Output Media File will be saved to the same location as the Source Media File.
  - *Desktop*: The Output Media File will be saved to the user's Desktop.
  - *User's Movie Folder*: The Output Media File will be saved to the user's Movie folder.
  - *Cluster Storage*: Available only if *Distributed Processing* is enabled for Compressor (see chapter about Render Farm).
- **Custom**: this folder contains all the custom Destinations that you create yourself.

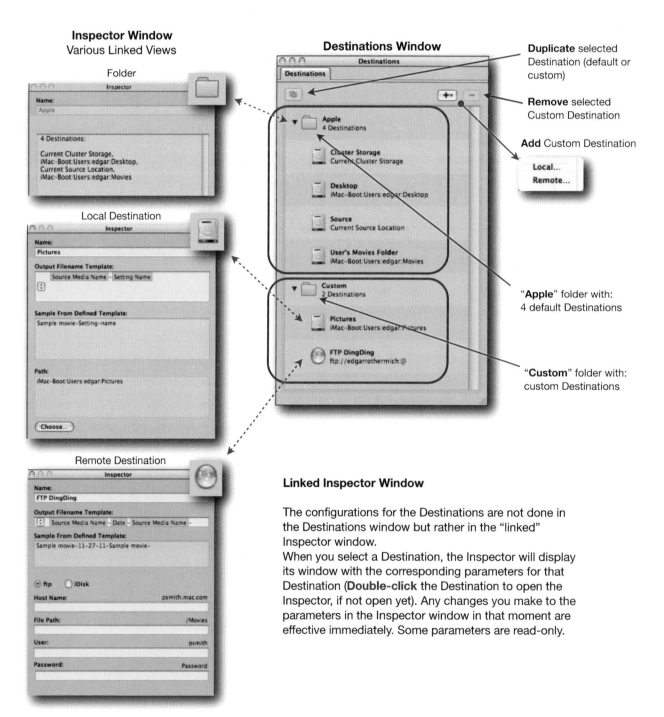

Inspector Window
Various Linked Views

Folder

Local Destination

Remote Destination

Destinations Window

Duplicate selected Destination (default or custom)

Remove selected Custom Destination

Add Custom Destination

"**Apple**" folder with: 4 default Destinations

"**Custom**" folder with: custom Destinations

Linked Inspector Window

The configurations for the Destinations are not done in the Destinations window but rather in the "linked" Inspector window.

When you select a Destination, the Inspector will display its window with the corresponding parameters for that Destination (**Double-click** the Destination to open the Inspector, if not open yet). Any changes you make to the parameters in the Inspector window in that moment are effective immediately. Some parameters are read-only.

There are two types of Destinations:

When you click on the plus button to create a new Destination , a popup menu lists these two choices: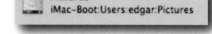

➡ Create a Local Destination

- Click the plus button and then select "*Local...*" from the popup menu.

- A File Selector Dialog will open. It lets you navigate to the location that you want to choose for your Destination. You can use any folder of any mounted drive, which can be a local drive or a network volume. Click the Open button.

- The File Selector Dialog closes and the new Destination will be created in the Custom folder of the Destinations window.

- The new Destination will be named after the Folder location you chose. The line underneath displays the path to that folder. The Local Destination will be represented by a hard drive icon.

- **Double-click** on the new Destination to open the Inspector Window to further configure it. The Inspector Window provides the following settings and controls:

> ❶ **Name**: This is the name of the Destination which was inherited from the defined folder location when it was created the first time. You can overwrite it.
>
> ❷ **Output Filename Template**: Set the rules on how to name the Output Media File (see below).
>
> ❸ **Sample From Defined Template**: This displays how the Name will look like based on the configured Filename Template (read only).
>
> ❹ **Path**: This is the full path to the defined folder location where the Output Media file will be saved.
>
> ❺ **Choose**: This button will open the File Selector Dialog again to choose a different folder location for the Destination.

Inspector - Local Destination

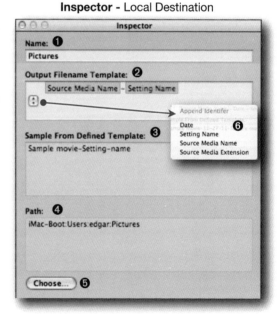

🙂 Filename Template

Every Destination contains two components: The actual Destination and the Name for the Output Media file. The first value is easy, because it is a fixed value, the Folder location. The Filename however cannot be fixed. Otherwise, all the Output Media Files would end up having the same name. Instead of a fixed value, you configure a set of rules with variables. This is called an "*Output Filename Template*". The process is fairly simple:

The Output Filename Template section in the Inspector is like a mini-scripting area. You click on it and a blinking text cursor will appear like in a text editor.

- You can enter plain text in the box, and/or ...

- Click on the little button to open the *Append Identifier* popup menu ❻. It lists four variables (the Identifiers) that you can place into the text box by clicking on it. For example, if you select "*Source Media Name*", then the name for the Output Media File will inherit whatever name the Source Media File has for this transcoding process. The script will automatically add a hyphen between two selected Identifiers. You can choose from:
  Date - **Setting Name** - **Source Media Name** - **Source Media Extension**

- Delete any plain text or any Identifier from the text box by placing the cursor right after it and hitting the **delete** key.

- Rearrange the Identifiers by dragging them to the correct position.

➡ Create a Remote Destination

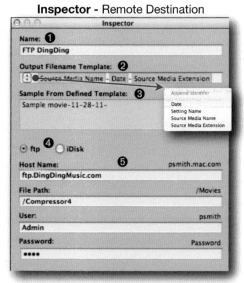

FTP DingDing
ftp://Admin:@ftp.DingDingMusic.com/Compressor4

- Click the plus button on the Destinations Window ➕▾ and then select "*Remote...*" from the popup menu.

- A sheet will slide out underneath the Destinations Window to configure the parameters for the Remote Destination.

- You can enter the parameters now or leave them for later. Click the "OK" button.

- The sheet closes and the new Remote Destination will be created in the Custom folder of the Destinations Window.

- The new Destination will display the name it was given in the previous window. The line underneath displays the ftp path. The Remote Destination will be represented by a globe icon.

- Open the Inspector Window to further configure the new Destination. The Inspector Window provides the following settings and controls:

> ❶ **Name**: This is the name of the Destination from the original configuration sheet. You can overwrite it.
>
> ❷ **Output Filename Template**: Set the rules on how to name the Output Media File (see explanation on the previous page).
>
> ❸ **Sample From Defined Template**: This displays how the Name will look based on the configured Filename Template (read only).
>
> ❹ **FTP / iDisk**: The radio buttons let you choose between the ftp and iDisk protocol. "iDisk" is a discontinued service by Apple, so this choice might disappear in a future Compressor update or perhaps be replaced with the iCloud service.
>
> ❺ **FTP login**: These four fields provide the login data for a specific ftp location. This is very convenient because you don't have to be logged in to the ftp server before the transcoding. Compressor is automatically logging in as part of the transcoding process. Set User and Password only if required by the FTP server.

Inspector - Remote Destination

Inspector

Name: ❶
FTP DingDing

Output Filename Template: ❷
Source Media Name - Date - Source Media Extension

Sample From Defined Template: ❸
Sample movie-11-28-11-

Append Identifier
Date
Setting Name
Source Media Name
Source Media Extension

❹
⊙ ftp ○ iDisk
Host Name: ❺   psmith.mac.com
ftp.DingDingMusic.com
File Path: /Movies
/Compressor4
User: psmith
Admin
Password: Password
••••

Filename Conflicts

Compressor warns you upfront if there are potential problems with the Destination or the Naming before you start the transcoding process. The Target will be marked with a yellow warning triangle or a red exclamation sign. When you move your mouse over a sign, a yellow helper tag appears briefly with information about the problem.

▸ ❶ A file with the same filename exists already in that Destination location. This is only a yellow warning sign. You can ignore it and Compressor will overwrite the existing file in that location.

▸ ❷ Two Targets have the same Name and Destination assigned. This could happen when you manually overwrite a Name. Compressor usually detects duplicate names and adds an incremental number to them. You will be prompted with an Alert window ❹ if you try to ignore this warning.

▸ ❸ This indicates any problems with the Destination volume, either a read-write issue or the configured volume is unmounted. You will be prompted with an Alert window ❺ if you try to ignore this warning.

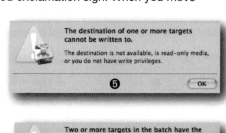

The destination of one or more targets cannot be written to.

The destination is not available, is read-only media, or you do not have write privileges.

❺   OK

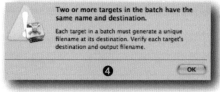

Two or more targets in the batch have the same name and destination.

Each target in a batch must generate a unique filename at its destination. Verify each target's destination and output filename.

❹   OK

Sky.MOV

iPhone HD ‖ Pictures ❶ ‖ Sky.m4v ⚠ ➖ ➕
iPhone HD ‖ Pictures ‖ SkyNew.m4v ❗ ➖ ➕
❷
iPhone HD ‖ Pictures ‖ SkyNew.m4v ❗ ➖ ➕
iPhone HD ❸‖ Documents ❗ ‖ SkyNew.Net.m4v ➖ ➕

This target will overwrite an existing file with the same name. To preserve the existing file, change the destination or change the name of the output file.

Two targets in the batch have the same name and destination. Change the destination or change the name of the output file.

The destination you have specified does not have read/write access. Check to see if the folder is set to read-only, or check your write privileges.

➡ **Select a Destination**

There are different ways to assign a Destination to a Target:

🌐 **Manual Select**

- Select the Target(s) or Job(s) and choose from the Main Menu *Target > Destination >* . This opens a submenu displaying all the available Destinations (Apple and Customs). You can choose any other location from the File Selector Dialog with the "Other... command.

- Select the Target(s) or Job(s) and **right+click** on it to use the Contextual Menu. This opens a submenu with the same items as the main menu.

🌐 **Drag**

- **Drag** a Destination from the Destinations Window directly onto a Target. This assigns it to that Target.

- **Drag** a Destination from the Destinations Window onto a Job. This creates an empty Target with that Destination.

- **Drag** a Destination from the Destinations Window onto a Batch. This creates a Job with an empty Target with that Destination.

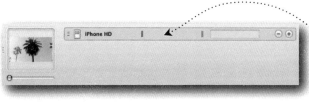

🌐 **Automatic**

Destinations will be assigned automatically under various circumstances. Keep an eye on three locations outside the Destinations Window that affect the automatic creation of Destinations:

❶ **Preferences**: You can select any of the available Destinations as the *Default Destination*.

❷ **Settings**: Each Setting can have a specific Destination assigned to it in the Actions tab of the Inspector.

❸ **Save Batch Template**: It provides a checkbox *"Use Compressor's default destination"*.

- Creating a new Setting will automatically assign its own Default Destination if it was configured. If it was set to "none", then no Destination will be assigned .

- If you use the *"New Target with Setting"* command:
  - The Target will assign that Setting with its Default Destination (if configured).
  - The Target will assign that Setting with the Default Destination selected from the Preferences. (if the Setting's Destination was set to "none)

- If you choose a New Batch Template.
  - If the checkbox ❸ was unchecked, then the Target will follow the Setting configuration (Destination selected or set to none)
  - If the checkbox was checked, then the Default Destination from the Preferences will be used, overwriting any Destination configuration from the Setting itself.

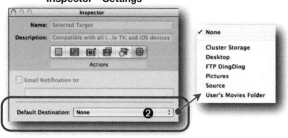

Either you can remember all those conditions or just configure the transcoding and change the Destination in the Target with a simple "Manual Select" or "Drag" the Destination you want.

Settings

Finally, the heart of Compressor, the Settings.

> ## Settings = Transcoding Instructions

A Setting is like a macro that contains a complete set of transcoding instructions.

- The Settings Window contains all the different Settings for different transcoding purposes.
- The Inspector Window lets you view and edit the individual configuration parameters of a Setting

There are two steps involved when using Settings:

Step ❶ - **ASSIGN**: Choose a Setting from the Settings Window and assign it to the Target.

> You always have to start with a preconfigured Setting. The Settings Window provides a wide variety of Settings for different kinds of needs and this might be all you need. You don't have to know anything about the details of the Settings. For example, if you want to transcode a big video file to play on an iPhone and the iPhone Setting is doing the job, then just assign that Setting to the Target and you are ready to go.

Step ❷ - **CONFIGURE**: Configure/tweak the Setting.

> If you are more of an adventures type of person, then you can go to Step 2 and adjust the Setting to your own liking. The linked Inspector Window is your editing tool. It lets you view and edit all the individual parameters that make up the Settings.

- **Create (2a)**: You can create your own Setting that you can use later. Maybe the default iPhone Settings was not quite right. Change it so it suits your needs and save it as your own custom Setting. From now on, you can assign that custom Setting to the Target whenever you need that custom iPhone transcoding.
- **Adjust (2b)**: You can also tweak a Setting that you have already assigned to the Target.

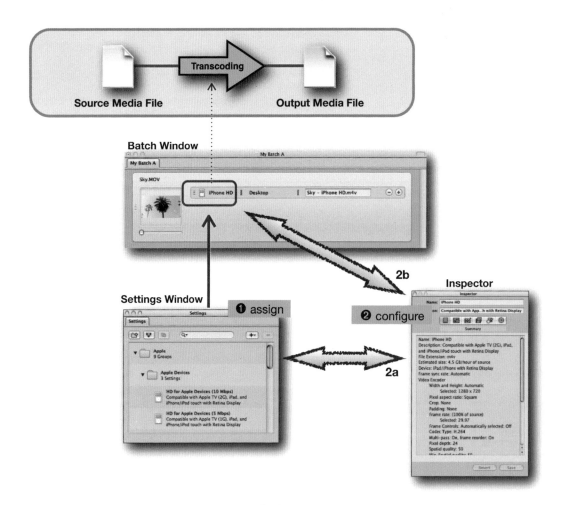

Manage Settings

The different Settings are managed in the Settings Window. The window only contains:

▶ The Header with various controls:

▶ The Settings List, organized in two folders:

- **Apple**: this folder contains all the default Settings that can't be changed or removed.
- **Custom**: this folder contains all the custom Settings that you create yourself.

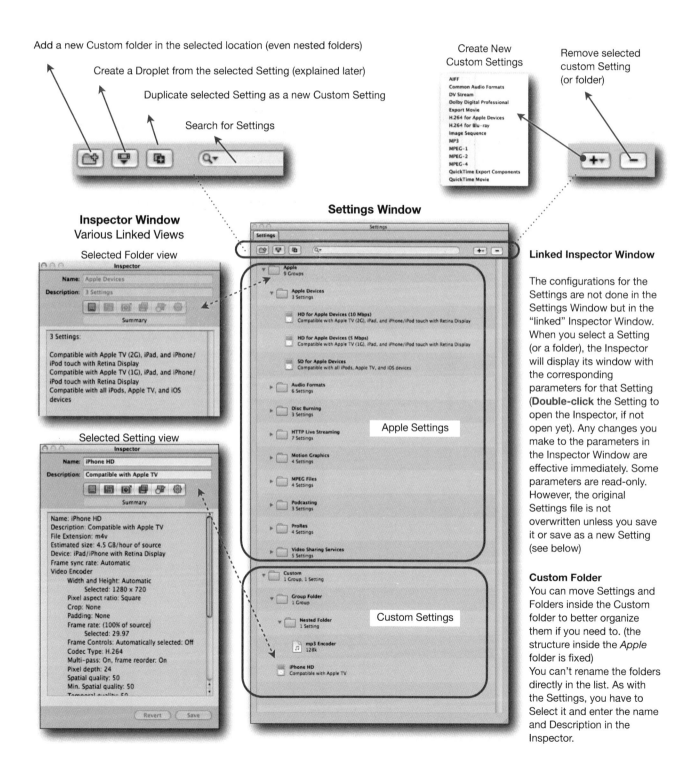

Add a new Custom folder in the selected location (even nested folders)

Create a Droplet from the selected Setting (explained later)

Duplicate selected Setting as a new Custom Setting

Search for Settings

Create New Custom Settings

Remove selected custom Setting (or folder)

Inspector Window
Various Linked Views

Selected Folder view

Settings Window

Linked Inspector Window

The configurations for the Settings are not done in the Settings Window but in the "linked" Inspector Window. When you select a Setting (or a folder), the Inspector will display its window with the corresponding parameters for that Setting (**Double-click** the Setting to open the Inspector, if not open yet). Any changes you make to the parameters in the Inspector Window are effective immediately. Some parameters are read-only. However, the original Settings file is not overwritten unless you save it or save as a new Setting (see below)

Custom Folder
You can move Settings and Folders inside the Custom folder to better organize them if you need to. (the structure inside the *Apple* folder is fixed)
You can't rename the folders directly in the list. As with the Settings, you have to Select it and enter the name and Description in the Inspector.

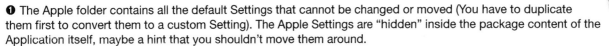

➡ Setting File

Each Setting in the Settings Window, unlike Destinations, is a representations of an actual file on the hard drive. An XML file with the file extension ".setting". There are two locations where those files are stored:

❶ The Apple folder contains all the default Settings that cannot be changed or moved (You have to duplicate them first to convert them to a custom Setting). The Apple Settings are "hidden" inside the package content of the Application itself, maybe a hint that you shouldn't move them around.

❷ The Custom folder contains all the Settings and nested Subfolders that you create. They are stored in a Settings folder in the user's Library folder and represent the exact file structure that you have in the Compressor's Settings Window. Those files and folders can be moved around in the Finder. See below.

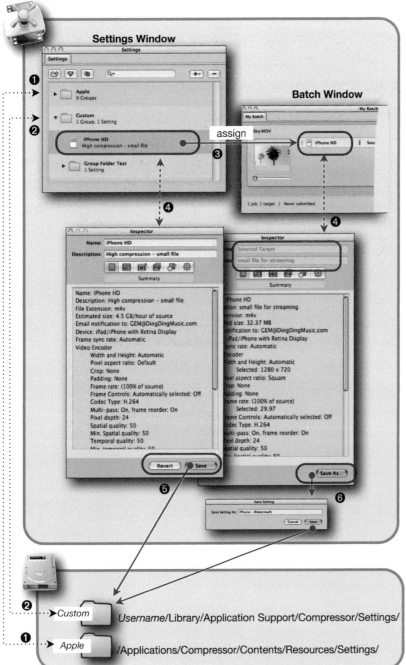

❸ While each Setting in the Settings Window is a representation of the actual Setting file, the Setting that you assign to a Target is not. When you assign a Setting to the Target, you make a copy of that Setting.

❹ This is important to understand when it comes to editing the parameters in the Inspector. There is a difference in the Inspector Window when you select a Setting from the Settings Window or a Setting assigned to a Target.

❺ When selecting a custom Setting from the Settings Window, all the parameters are available. In addition, at the bottom are two buttons:
- **Revert**: This resets all the parameters to the values which were stored in that Setting.
- **Save**: This overwrites the Setting file with any changes you made.

A dialog window will pop up when you leave the Inspector view after you've made unsaved changes to the Setting. Once again, the same Save or Revert options are available.

❻ When selecting a Setting on a Target, a few things are different:
- The Name of the Setting is replaced with "*Selected Target*"
- The Name and Description field are grayed out and cannot be changed
- The bottom of the Inspector now only has one button **Save as...** This lets you create a new Setting based on the current parameter values, in case you want to use that Setting later. A dialog window will pop up that lets you enter a name for that new Setting. Please note that the current Setting in the Target is now a copy of the newly created Setting which has been added to the Settings Window.

➡ Ways to move around

One more step before looking at the actual parameters of a Setting. With the understanding of the connection between the listed Settings in the Settings Window and their relationship to their Setting File, let's look at all possible ways we can move those Settings around.

☻ Assigning Settings

The first type of "moving" is the assignment of a Setting to a Target. Remember this is a "one-way" copy process of the Setting to the Target. There are different ways for this action:

Menu Selection:

▹ Select one or many Targets in one Batch Window and go to the Main Menu *Target > Change Setting....* That slides out a sheet under the Batch Window which contains the same Settings as the Settings Window. It even provides a search box.

▹ Select one or many Targets in one Batch Window and **right+click** to select from the Contextual Menu *Change Setting... >.* This slides out the same sheet.

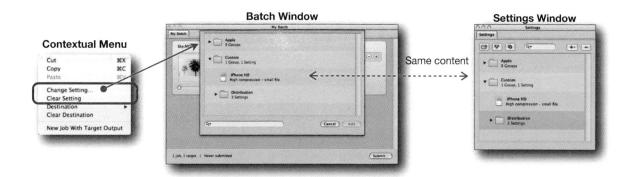

▹ The contextual menu also contains the command to remove a Setting from a Target *"Clear Setting"*

Dragging Settings

You can drag a Setting from the Settings Window onto the Target. In addition to that, you can even drag a Setting file directly from the Finder onto the Target. There are three areas in the Batch Window where you can drag the Settings to:

▹ Dragging onto the Target: Assigns that Setting to that Target.

▹ Dragging onto a Job: Creates a new Target with that Setting in the Job. It even allows the dragging of multiple Settings to create multiple new Targets at once.

▹ Dragging onto a Batch: Creates an empty Job with one Target that has that Setting assigned to it. Also allows the dragging of multiple Settings to create multiple new Targets at once.

Dragging a Folder (Groups)

If you have a workflow that require the transcoding of files into multiple Output Files (High Res, Low Res, Streaming, etc), then you can place all those Settings into one Group Folder in the Settings Window and drag that folder onto a Job or Batch (not on a single Target). This creates one Target for each Setting in the Group Folder.

🦴 Managing Settings

The following actions and commands are for the Settings. It shows the flexibility of Compressor when it comes to organizing your Setting

- In the Settings Window
    - ▶ Create New Settings (and group folders)
    - ▶ Duplicate Existing Setting
    - ▶ Drag Settings and Folders around

- Between Settings Window - Finder Window
    - ▶ You can drag Settings from the Settings Window to the Finder. This creates a Setting file with the name of the Setting and the extension ".setting".
    - ▶ You can also drag the other way around, a Setting file from the Finder onto the Settings Window. You can drag it onto the Custom folder or any nested folder inside. Please note that you can rename the Setting file in the Finder but this is not the actual name of the Setting that will be displayed when you drag it into the Settings Window. The Setting name is stored inside that XML file.

- Custom Folder location
    - ▶ As we have seen on the previous page, all the custom Settings are stored in a specific folder in the user's Library. You can copy those files between different machines to exchange Settings.
    - ▶ You can rearrange the Setting files and the nested folders in that specific Setting folder (while Compressor is NOT running). The next time you start Compressor, that new file structure is represented in the Settings Window.

🦴 Extract Settings

This is a really cool feature. Imagine a Media File carrying its own "Transcoding Fingerprint" beyond the standard Metadata. Maybe you have a video file (your own or from someone else) that looks really good and has a small file size. You wonder what kind of compression parameters are used to create this specific file - Compressor can tell you:

- ▶ Drag the Media File from the Finder onto the Settings Window.
- ▶ Compressor creates a Setting with the name "Untitled" and the name of the Media File in the second line (which is the Description).
- ▶ Select the Settings and the Inspector Window displays all the parameters it could extract from that file.

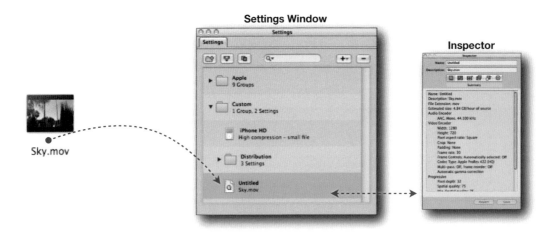

Edit Settings

All the parameters and attributes for a Setting are displayed and can be changed in the Inspector Window. It also provides the controls to save a Setting as a Setting File. Make sure you know whether you have selected a Setting from the Settings Window or from the Target of a Batch. There are a few minor differences.

▶ **Name**: This is the name of the Settings that you can enter. This name will be displayed in the Settings list in bold. If the Inspector displays a Target's Settings, then the field is grayed out and displays "Selected Target".

▶ **Description**: Here you can enter a short description for the Setting. This entry will be displayed as the second line for a Setting in the Settings Window. For a selected Target Setting, this field is also grayed out.

▶ **Tab Selector**: These 6 tabs select what is displayed in the main window pane below. The little box below the tabs displays the name of the currently selected tab.

▶ **Parameters Pane**: this window segment displays the parameters and attributes depending on the selected tab.

▶ **Save buttons**: it displays either a "*Save as...*" button if a Target's Setting is selected or a "*Revert*" and "*Save*" button if a Setting is selected from the Settings Window. The buttons are only active if there have been any changes made to the Setting.

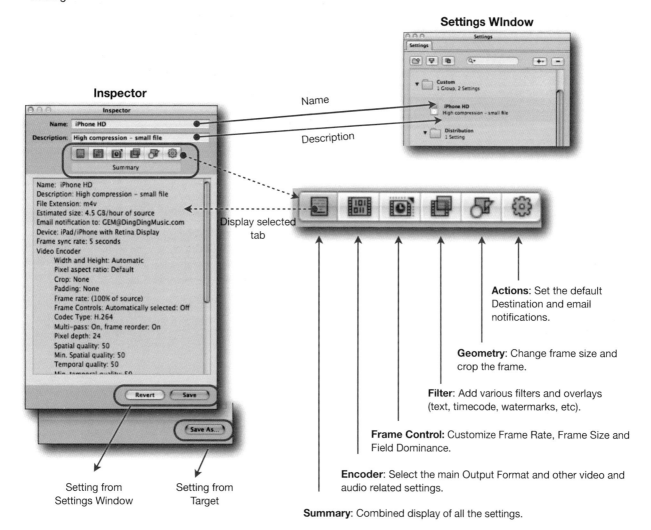

Actions: Set the default Destination and email notifications.

Geometry: Change frame size and crop the frame.

Filter: Add various filters and overlays (text, timecode, watermarks, etc).

Frame Control: Customize Frame Rate, Frame Size and Field Dominance.

Encoder: Select the main Output Format and other video and audio related settings.

Summary: Combined display of all the settings.

- The Inspector Window is the only window in Compressor that cannot be resized. All content for the various control tabs are displayed in the window pane below.

- The four sections, Encoder, Frame Control, Filter and Geometry are somehow connected. Some settings for a specific control in one section could influence another section.

- The Geometry section is linked to the Preview Window as discussed in the Preview chapter.

The Automatic Mode:

Compressor provides an automatic mode for some parameters, indicated by the Automatic Button ❶. If active, the best value for that specific item is determined by Compressor automatically. In that case, the active button is dark and the popup menu is dimmed, displaying the automatic value. However, if no Source File has been assigned to the Job yet or the Inspector displays a Setting from the Settings Window, then the popup menu displays "Automatic" ❷.

 **Summary**

The Summary pane is a read only section and no selections can be made there. It displays all the parameter configurations made under the five tabs.

 **Encoder**

The Encoder contains the most important configurations. It sets the file format that the transcoded file will have.

The popup menu lists 14 different file formats. Each file format switches to a different window layout with controls specific for that particular File Format. The official Compressor manual provides a detailed explanations of the controls for each of the different File Formats.

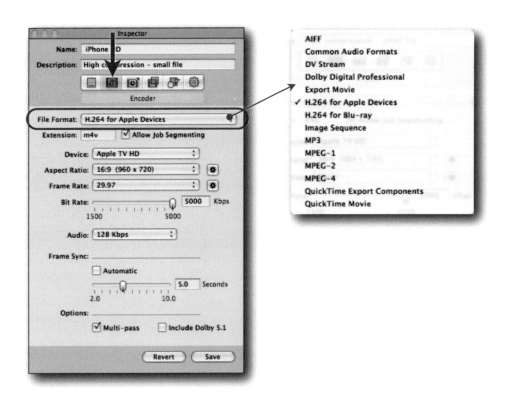

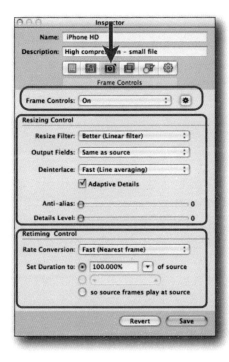 **Frame Controls**

The Frame Control section always has the same layout regardless of the selected File Format in the Encoder pane. However, if the Frame Control settings don't apply to a specific file format (i.e. Audio formats), then the controls are dimmed and inactive.
The whole section can be turned on and off with the first item: Frame Controls: on/off.
The following controls are divided into two sections: Resizing Controls and Retiming Controls.

Those controls are for advanced image analyses that used to require expensive hardware components. i.e.:
- Video standards conversion like PAL to NTSC
- Interlaced to progressive video
- Up-converting and down-converting
- Reverse Telecine
- Slow motion effects

The affect of any of the Frame Controls' settings cannot be previewed in the Preview Window.

The official Apple manual for Compressor 4 provides a detailed explanation of all the advanced Frame Control settings.

 Filter

The Filter section has a lot of useful little features and tools that go beyond the actual "filtering". This is a perfect example of using the Inspector Window in conjunction with the Preview Window because you can immediately see how the effect will look. You can then fine tune it before committing to the final transcoding process.
The layout of the Filter section is divided into three areas:

▶ ❶ Tabs: Video - Audio - Color
The tab selects which specific controls are displayed.

▶ ❷ Filter selection
The available filters and tools for the selected tab are listed with a checkbox that lets you temporarily enable or disable individual filters.

▶ ❸ The window pane below provides the actual controls for the selected filter

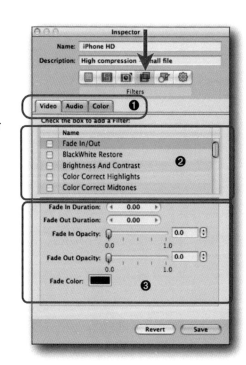

Some examples:
- Apply a video fade in and out
- Add some text overlays or watermark logos
- Generate visual Timecode
- Apply de-interlacing
- Simple color corrections
- Apply audio compression and/or limiting to quickly enhance the audio loudness
- Apply audio EQ with a graphic equalizer
- Apply audio fade in and fade out

 **Geometry**

The previous panes are either explained in detail in the official manual or they are self explanatory if you're playing around with them a little bit. The Geometry pane however is slightly different. It looks easy, but there are a lot of little details that can lead to confusion or even worse, to the wrong assumption and therefore to wrong transcoding results. That's why I want to delve deeper into that section.

For this pane, it is definitely a good practice, to have the Preview Window open to get visual feedback concerning the outcome of the various settings. I already covered some of the concepts in the Preview chapter and want to build on that.

The most important button in the Preview Window is in the upper right corner, the "View Frame Size" button. It has to be set correctly in order to display the Preview video frame in the actual Frame Size of the "to be transcoded" Output Media File. Please note that changes you make in the Geometry pane don't always get displayed in the Preview Window right away. This could lead to a wrong display of the actual data. To "update" the Preview Window manually, just toggle those two buttons back and forth.

The Geometry Pane has three sections:

❶ Cropping

These settings affect the actual content of the video. You set the values (or the corresponding cropping boundaries in the Preview Window) to cut out a portion of the original video frame. A popup menu ("Crop to") provides some crop preset settings based on common video standards. I discussed that earlier in the Preview chapter.

❷ Output Frame Size

Although labeled "Dimensions", this section defines the actual Frame Size of the Output Media File. This Frame Size setting, displayed in Width and Height is also shown in the left lower corner of the Preview Window when set to "Output Frame Size" (see the Preview chapter for details).
One important step that can be easily overlooked, the "Scaling" process, is not listed in the Geometry pane. Compressor makes the original Frame Size (Source media minus Cropping setting) "fit" into the new Frame Size chosen in this section. Different Aspect Ratios could lead to squeezed or stretched video (see also the Preview chapter for examples)

❸ Padding

Padding allows black bars to be added on each side. Very important, this doesn't change the Frame Size of the Output file set in the previous sections. Any padding will therefore shrink the actual video content. This could result in an additional Aspect Ratio mismatch. Some settings from the popup menu make it possible to compensate for an existing Aspect Ratio mismatch due to the previous scaling process.

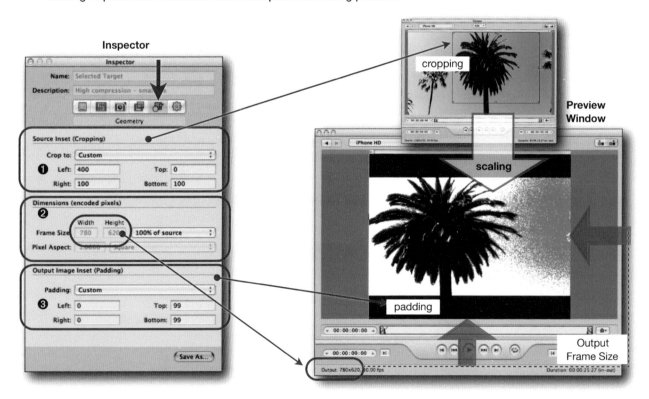

Here is an attempt to illustrate the various Frame Size controls and their connections with a flow chart diagram.

▶ At the top is the original Frame Size of the Source Media File ❶.

▶ That Frame Size is "feeding" the Geometry pane with its three modules, Cropping, Output, Padding

▶ The red arrows don't represent the signal flow of the video signal. They illustrate the Frame Size controls (and the Filter pane controls) which affect the size and how the video signal will look.

▶ The blue boxes represent the Preview Window with its split screen (a "Setting" is selected in the Preview's Batch Item popup menu). The left portion displays all the controls affecting the Source Media file ❷ and the right portion the Output Media file ❸. The two Preview frames on the left and right represent one frame of the Preview Window, but I arranged them separately for clarity purposes.

▶ The arrows that point from the top down to the Preview frame represent the state when the left "Frame Size View" button is selected (Source) ❹. The arrows that point upwards to the Preview frame represent the state when the right "Frame Size View" buttons are selected (Setting) ❺.

▶ The Cropping module in the Geometry section is linked to the Cropping Boundaries in the Preview Window ❻. You can make the adjustment in either window.

▶ The "invisible" part in the Geometry pane is the Scaling. Think of a formula like:
"SourceFrameSize" minus "Cropping" >>> (scaled to) OutputFrameSize".

▶ The output (Frame Size) of the Output module is controlling the left portion of the split screen (Source Media) ❼. The control for the right portion the Preview's split screen (Output Media) is going through the Padding module first ❽.

▶ Any settings made in the Filter pane ❾ are always visible in the right portion of the Preview's split screen (Output Media).

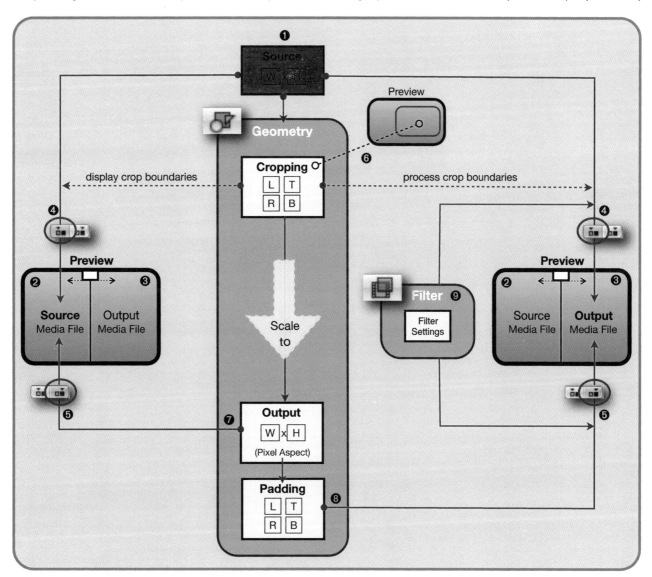

➡ Cropping section

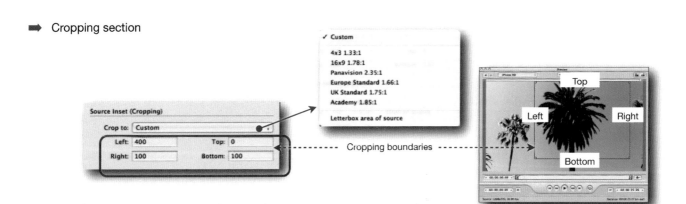

The *"Crop to"* popup menu contains:

- The *Custom* item. This lets you manually enter a pixel offset for any of the four sides of the frame. Only when *Custom* is selected, can you drag the cropping boundaries in the Preview Window (visible if the Frame Size selector is set to Source, left button). Changing the values in one window will update the other.

- The rest of the popup menu provide cropping presets based on common video standards and their Aspect Ratio. The Cropping boundaries are set so they use the maximum Width or Height of the Source Media's Frame Size, depending on the Aspect Ratio. The "Letterbox area of source" setting detects any black bars in a letterbox image and sets the cropping boundaries to cut them out. Choosing any of those non-Custom settings will disable the manual adjustment handles on the cropping boundaries in the Preview Window. The four value boxes display the cropping amount. However, they are grayed out and can't be changed, unless you switch to *Custom* again.

➡ Output

In the Preview chapter, I discussed the details of Frame Size, Aspect Ratio and related terminology. Now, we are confronted with the term "Dimensions" ❷ in the Inspector . Technically, the Dimensions of a video are the same as the Frame Size of a video. Both are displayed with the "width x height" value. The unit for the width and height is pixel. The sometimes overlooked detail is that pixels can have a different shape in different video standards. That means that a video frame with square shaped pixels has a different Dimension than a video frame with rectangle shaped pixels, even if they both are listed with the same "width x height" Frame Size.

That's why the Dimensions section of the Geometry pane has two settings, the Frame Size and the Pixel Aspect.

▸ Pixel Aspect: The popup menu provides all different kinds of standards to choose from. For digital video on computer screens, the setting defaults to *Square* shaped pixels.

▸ Frame Size: The popup menu provides a long list with all different kinds of sizes. They are organized in groups. Whatever you select, the actual width and height value is displayed in the two boxes to he left:

- Automatic: Compressor chooses the best value.

- Fixed Percentage: choose from same size, half size and quarter size of the Source Media's Frame Size.

- Up to Maximum width or height:. Choosing any of those frame size values makes sure that either the width or the height doesn't exceed that value while keeping the original Aspect Ratio.

- Fixed Aspect Ratio: choose from 7 common Frame Sizes 320x240 up to 1920x1080. This could potentially change the Aspect Ratio of the Source Media file.

- Custom: This lets you enter any width and height value without restrictions.

- Custom (plus fixed Aspect Ratio): You can enter/change the width or height and the other value will automatically be set to conform to the listed Aspect Ratio.

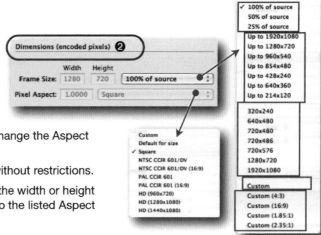

Please note that the displayed value for width and height is most of the time the final Frame Size of the Output Media file, but there are exceptions with specific combinations from the cropping settings. The exact value is displayed in the left lower corner of the Preview Window. This is the actual pixel Dimension of the image frame. How much video content is visible depends on the Padding settings.

➡ Padding

Padding is the extra blank space in form of black bars. This has the effect that the frame size of the video image (the actual video content) is smaller than the frame size of the video file itself.

This section provides a popup menu and the four entry boxes for the padding value on each side of the video frame. The important thing to know is that the Frame Size of the Output Media file will not be changed, just the size and shape of the video image (the visual video picture). If the video image is identical with the Frame Size then there is no padding. Any padding value will shrink the video image. The question is if the video image maintains its Aspect Ratio or gets squeezed/streched resulting in a distorted view of the video image.

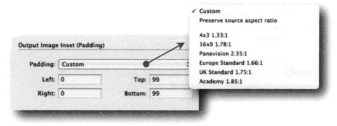

▶ *Custom*: With this selection, you can freely enter any padding value on the four sides.

▶ Preserve source aspect ratio: This is a really helpful setting which fixes any Aspect Ratio problems that result from the selection of the previous settings in the Geometry pane. We saw earlier that a key element in the Geometry pane is the Scaling. Whatever cropping setting and new Frame Size for the Output file you choose, the original Frame Size of the Source Media file will be scaled to those dimensions regardless of the Aspect Ratio. An often unwanted side effect is a squeezed or stretched video image. The "Preserve source aspect ratio" setting now shrinks the video image to the nearest level so it fits into the Frame Size. Any space will be filled with padded black bars to maintain the actual Frame Size for the Output Media file.

▶ Various Video standards: This forces the video image into the Aspect Ratio of various picture standards resulting in a stretched or squeezed picture if the Aspect Ratio is different from the Source Media file. Black bars will be added to maintain the Frame Size of the Output Media file.

 Action

The Action section provides only two controls:

▶ **Email Notification**: This is a post-transcoding action. It determines what happens after the transcoding process is done. In this case, an email will be sent to the address that you enter in the box.

▶ **Default Destination**: I discussed this feature in the context of Destinations Window in the Destination chapter. From the popup menu, you select which Destination will be automatically assigned to a Target that has this Setting selected.

History Window

The History Window is not linked to any other window. You can open it from the Windows menu or by using the button in the Toolbar of a Batch Window (if visible). The History Window opens automatically if you submit a Batch. It provides the following functionality:

- View a progress bar displaying ongoing transcoding processes (remaining time).
- Pause ongoing transcoding processes.
- View submission details.
- View Info about previously submitted batches.
- Locate Output Media files.
- Resubmit a batch by dragging it from the History Window onto the Batch Window.

History Window

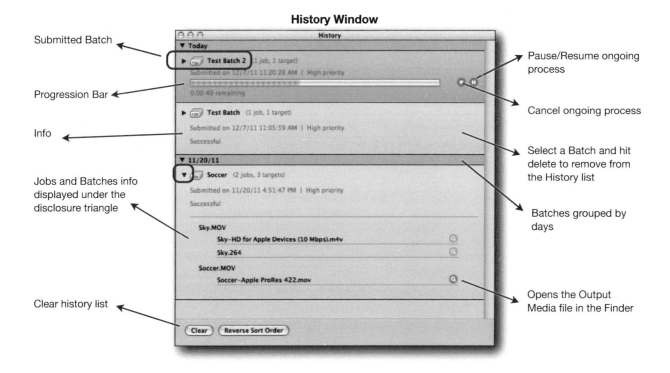

Submitted Batch

Progression Bar

Info

Jobs and Batches info displayed under the disclosure triangle

Clear history list

Pause/Resume ongoing process

Cancel ongoing process

Select a Batch and hit delete to remove from the History list

Batches grouped by days

Opens the Output Media file in the Finder

Share Monitor

Although the Share Monitor window provides functionality that is similar to the History Window, it isn't another Compressor window, but rather a separate application. Like a print utilitiy that displays all the print jobs from various applications and even different computers on the network, Share Monitor displays processing jobs from Final Cut Pro, Motion, Apple Qmaster and Apple QAdministrator, even submitted from other computers.

Unlike the History Window, Share Monitor doesn't keep past Batch processes after Compressor and Share Monitor quit. It is also not possible to drag a Batch from the Share Monitor back to the Batch Window for re-processing.

Two ways to open the Share Monitor in Compressor:

- Click on the button in the Batch Window's Toolbar (if visible)
- Have it automatically open when you submit a batch. This behavior can be activated from the Compressor's Preferences window with the checkbox "*Automatically open Share Monitor*".

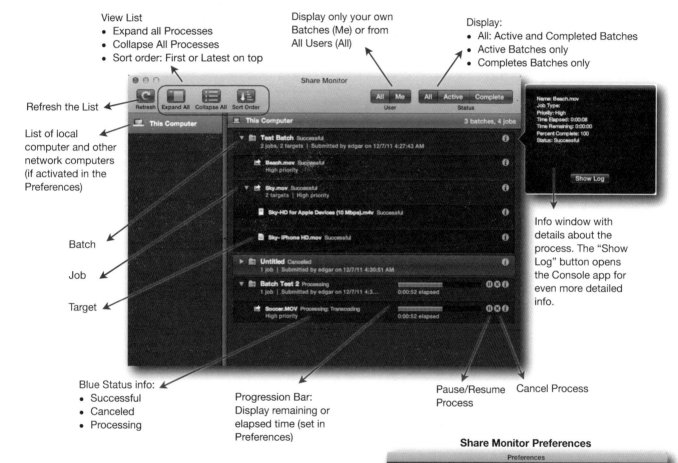

View List
- Expand all Processes
- Collapse All Processes
- Sort order: First or Latest on top

Display only your own Batches (Me) or from All Users (All)

Display:
- All: Active and Completed Batches
- Active Batches only
- Completes Batches only

Refresh the List

List of local computer and other network computers (if activated in the Preferences)

Batch

Job

Target

Info window with details about the process. The "Show Log" button opens the Console app for even more detailed info.

Blue Status info:
- Successful
- Canceled
- Processing

Progression Bar: Display remaining or elapsed time (set in Preferences)

Pause/Resume Process

Cancel Process

The Preference window provides additional settings for:

- ☑ **View Options**: Display Jobs, Targets and Segments
- ☑ **Network Options**: Add other network computers that should be displayed in the list for monitoring. This list corresponds to the Network Options setting in the Compressor's Preference Window.

Compressor Preferences

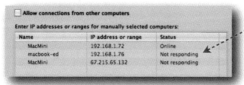

Share Monitor Preferences

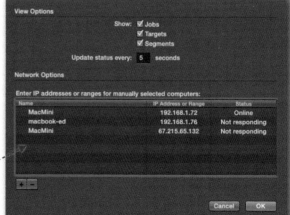

Other Topics

Submit

We discussed pretty much all aspects of the transcoding configuration so far except the actual step of pressing the Submit button on a Batch Window. That button doesn't start the transcoding process immediately. When looking closely at the button, we see that it is a *"Submit ..."* button. The three dots indicate that an extra configuration window will follow, a sheet that slides out underneath the Batch Window.

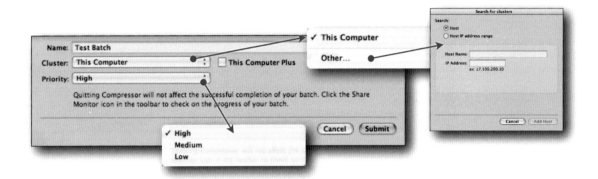

There are four configurations to be checked before hitting the Submit button again. This time the Submit button doesn't have dots, which means this is the final action button that starts the transcoding process.

After that, Compressor is not involved anymore and you could quit the program. Compressor is technically just a configuration app, it lets you do everything to get the files ready for the proper transcoding. The transcoding process itself is handled then by background processes on the machine or many machines combined as a cluster. More about that in the last chapter about rendering.

Here are the final configuration steps:

▶ Name:

This is not the Batch name. It is a new name to identify the processing job. When the window opens, the name is set to *"untitled"*. You only need to give it a name when you have many different transcoding processes going on and you want to identify them in the History or Share Monitor window later.

▶ Cluster

This popup menu decides 'who" should process the Batch.

- **This Computer**: Only the local computer will do the processing
- **A Cluster**: This is an optional list item. Only if a computer cluster has been configured as part of the Apple Qmaster, system, it will be displayed in this list and you can select that cluster to perform the processing.
- **Other...**: The following window lets you search for a cluster by name or IP address in case the cluster isn't displayed in the list.

▶ This Computer Plus

This checkbox creates a QuickCluster that doesn't require much knowledge and understanding of the distributed network. When checked, Compressor looks on the network to see if there are other Computers on the network that were configured to accept "render duties". See the next chapter for details.

▶ Priority

You can choose from three levels, High - Medium - Low. The default setting is *High* and you only need to choose a lower setting when you have many transcoding processes in your queue and want to set a priority among them.

Inspector

I covered the Inspector in detail already in the chapter about Settings and Destinations. This is just a summary with a few additional pieces of information.

The Inspector can be linked to three different windows, displaying the data of the selected object in that window

➡ Destinations Window

➡ Settings Window

➡ Batch Window

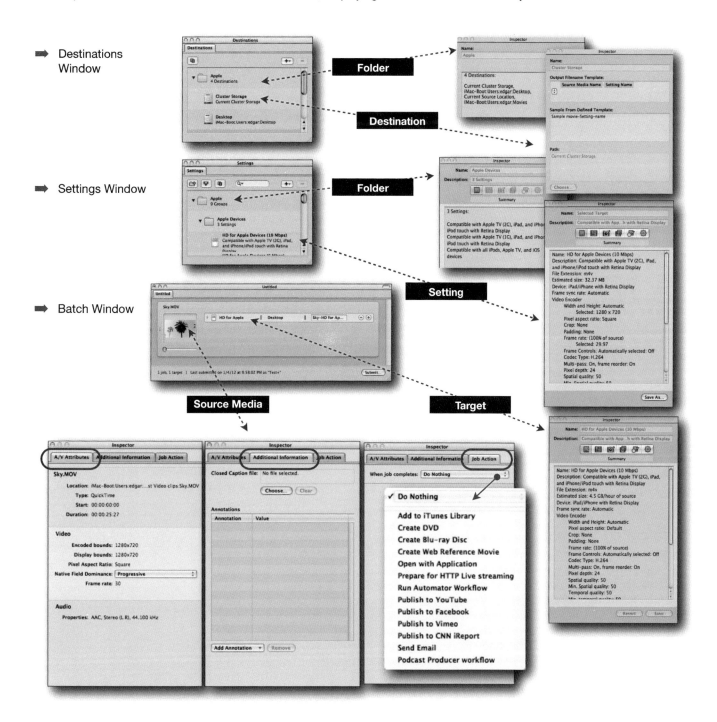

When a Source Media File is selected inside a Job, then the Inspector displays its window with three tabs:

- **A/V Attributes**: Displays audio and video attributes of the selected file. The window and its available attributes are different depending on the three media file types: Media File, Surround Sound Group, Image Sequence.

- **Additional Information**: Information for Closed Captions and Annotations.

- **Job Action**: You can select different actions from the popup menu that determine what happens after the transcoding job is completed. The window provides additional configurations depending on the selected action.

FCP Handshake

As I mentioned earlier, Compressor became more important with the release of FCPx. Here are a few reasons:

- Some features disappeared in the new FCPx and now require the use of Compressor (chapter markers, partial export of a project, etc).
- Specific export formats and settings are not available in FCPx.
- "Outsourcing" the export process to Compressor allows for more flexibility.
- Compressor provides the integration of clusters and network rendering.

There are three ways to hand over a project from FCPx to Compressor. They are all listed in the FCPx Share menu:

❶ Send a FCPx Project directly to Compressor.

❷ Export a Project in FCPx using one of the Compressor Settings.

❸ Choose any of the FCPx Export features, but use Compressor for the actual processing.

Let's look the details for the three procedures:

➡ Send to Compressor

This procedure requires three easy steps in FCPx. After that, you continue the setup in Compressor.

Step 2:
Select from the Main Menu
Share > Send to Compressor...

Step 1:
Select the Project in FCPx

Step 3:
This command will open Compressor with a new "*Untitled*" Batch and one Job. The Job is named after the FCPx Project and the thumbnail displays the FCPx logo.

➡ Export Using Compressor Settings

Using the previous "Send to Compressor" command requires the Compressor app. It will launch and you then have to continue to do more steps for the final transcoding procedure. However, if you have already setup your own Compressor settings that you want to use or want to use one of the default settings in Compressor, then you can do that without the need of Compressor. FCPx can access all of the Compressor Settings and use them for the export. As we have seen in the Settings chapter, the Settings are just XML files in a specific Compressor directory. FCPx "knows" where they are and "borrows" them for its own export process. Here are the steps:

▶ Select the command from the Main Menu *Share > Export Using Compressor Settings*

▶ A configuration window opens up:

☑ You can skim through the project's video thumbnail.

☑ You can search for a specific Settings.

☑ Select a Settings. The Summary tab will display the Output Media file's properties.

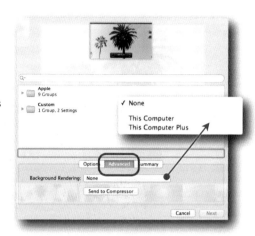

☑ Select the Advanced tab and choose one of the options:

- Background Rendering: Select **None**.
  Now click *Next* to let FCPx do the export with the selected Settings in the foreground.

- Background Rendering: Select **This Computer**.
  Now click *Next* to let the local computer perform the export in the background with the selected Setting.

- Background Rendering: Select **This Computer Plus**:
  Now click *Next* to let the local computer and any available render computer perform the export in the background with the selected Setting.

- Click the *Send to Compressor* button
  This is the same command as in the Share menu with the advantage that the newly created Batch in Compressor will have the selected Settings already assigned to the Job.

➡ Use FCPx Export with Advanced options

Selecting any of the FCPx export options in the Share menu will open up a configuration window with the various parameters. All the windows with the exception of the "Export..." option, have the same "Advanced" tab that we just saw in the configuration window for the "Export Using Compressor Settings".

There are three different scenarios:

▶ Background Rendering: None
FCPx will perform the export process in the foreground. That means that you have to wait until the export is finished before you can continue your work in FCPx.

▶ Background Rendering: **This Computer** or **This Computer Plus**
Choosing any of those two options will perform the export in the background, either on the local machine or the local machine and any available computer configured for rendering.

▶ Send to Compressor
This will open Compressor with a new Batch and the FCPx Project as the new Job. The selected export option in the FCPx Share menu will become the Settings. The advantage of this that you can fine tune the export settings and use parameters that might not be available in the FCPx Export window.

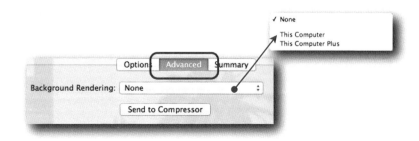

Droplets

A Droplet is a handy feature when you do a lot of transcoding with the same Settings. Here is the procedure:

➡ Create Droplet

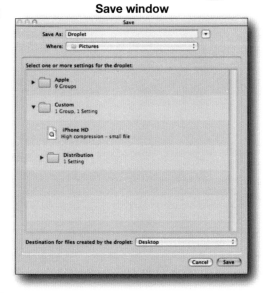

Save window

- Select the command from the Main Menu *File > Create Droplet ...* This will open a special File Selector Dialog window.
- Set four parameters:
    - ☑ Name the Droplet
    - ☑ Select a Finder location where to save the Droplet
    - ☑ Select a Setting
    - ☑ Select a Destination
- Click *Save*. This creates the Droplet. Please note that a Droplet is actually a little independent application by itself not just a configuration file. It has nothing to do with the Compressor app anymore.

From now on, drag any Source Media File(s) in the Finder directly on the Droplet to transcode it based on the configuration in the Droplet setup. You don't need to open Compressor at all because the transcoding is done by background processes and not Compressor itself (you can see them in the Activity Monitor application when you search for "*compressord*").

It is also possible to exchange the Droplet with other users on other computers.

➡ Modify Droplet

The editing of Droplets is a little bit unconventional:

Double-clicking on a Droplet will open the Droplet app with one window displaying the instructions for that Droplet.

To edit a different Droplet, you have to quit the Droplet app or close the window which will also quit the app. Now you can double-click on a different Droplet to open the Droplet app again, now with those instructions.

In the Droplet Window, you can do the following:

Droplet Window (app)

- You can change the defined Settings and Destination of a Droplet without having to create a new one. No need to save the changes. Quitting the Droplet app will automatically save the latest configuration for that Droplet.
- You can add additional Targets to the Droplet (the original *Create Droplet* command only allows one Target).
- You can add one or many Source Media files to the window and submit that whole Batch. Each Source Media File on the left would represent one Job with all the Targets on the right assigned to it.
- The plus and minus buttons let you add or remove Targets. Each Target can have its own Settings and Filename Template assigned to it. The only restriction is that you can choose only one Destination for a whole Droplet.
- The "I" button displays more info about the Setting and the *Show Details* button slides out a drawer with additional configurations for the selected Settings type.

Preferences

Here are all the settings in the Preferences window. Some of them I already covered in previous chapters.

Email Notification:
Compressor can send you an email to notify you when a transcoding process has been finished. This is especially useful when dealing with longer processes, multiple batches or if you need to notify your clients as a soon as a file is ready. Enter the email address and the SMTP domain of the outgoing mail server that handles the email. You can enter multiple email addresses separated by commas.

Automatically launch Share Monitor
When checked, the Share Monitor app will launch automatically when you submit a Batch to monitor the process.

Display job thumbnails
Compressor automatically activates this checkbox at launch, even if it was unchecked before. And even if you uncheck it, a thumbnail of the Source Media file is always displayed in the Job section. (Bug or obsolete checkbox?)

Various Cluster settings.
See the last chapter about Rendering for details

Preferences Window

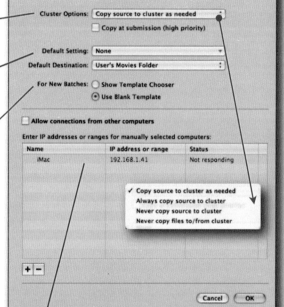

Default Setting / Default Destination
From the popup menus, choose a Setting that is used for a new Batch without a predefined Settings configuration and choose a Destination that is used for a Target without a predefined Destination configuration.

Batch Template Chooser
When you open Compressor the first time, a Template Chooser will be displayed to select a Batch Template. The window has a checkbox at the bottom where you can select "Don't show this dialog again". This will set the radio button in the Preference window to "Use Blank Template". Setting it back to "Show Template Chooser" will activate the Template Chooser dialog window again to be displayed at launch or whenever you create a new Batch.

Share Monitor
It is not really obvious, but this section relates to the Share Monitor application. The checkbox allows processing jobs on other machines to be displayed in the local Share Monitor application. The table below lets you add which machine on the network you want to monitor.

Dolby Digital

Dolby Digital is a special audio format sometimes referred to as AC-3. First of all, it is encoded, and playing it back requires a dedicated Dolby Digital decoder. The format provides compressed multi-channel surround sound that is used mainly for movies on DVDs, Blu-rays and also in movie theaters. But you are not limited to a DVD or Blu-ray to use this format. You can also create a Quicktime movie file with embedded audio in Dolby Digital surround sound.

Decoder

The mp3 is also a popular encoded audio format that requires a decoder. Typically mp3 decoders are included in most computer applications that deal with audio. Dolby Digital decoders are built into virtually every DVD and Blu-ray player. However, they are not common in computer applications. You can't playback an AC-3 file in iTunes for example. This creates a problem when you transcode any audio job to the Dolby Digital format. You would have to burn a disc first and play it through your disc player with a Dolby Decoder, hooked up to a surround sound system.

Another option is to play the AC-3 file (or a Quicktime file with Dolby Digital) through the optical out of your Mac that is connected to an external Dolby Digital decoder (see illustration below)

But here is an easier solution:

> Compressor4 has a built in Dolby Digital decoder.

This enables you to do two things:

▶ **Preview an AC-3 file**

Select an AC-3 file as the Source Media file in a Job and play it back with the controls of the Preview Window.

▶ **Convert an AC-3 file**

Select an AC-3 file as the Source Media file in a Job to transcode it to a different audio format. For example, if you have a QuickTime file that was encoded in AC-3 and you need to convert it to a plain aiff or mp3 audio format for playback compatibility reasons.

Playback AC-3 format.

Please note: AC-3 is a multichannel audio format. That means, it can include more than two audio channels. You have to keep in mind that although Compressor can decode those AC-3 files, if you don't have a multichannel speaker setup connected to your computer, you won't hear the surround sound properly. In that case, Compressor will down-mix the multichannel format to 2-channel stereo to play it back on the stereo speakers (either built in or external).

Here is an illustration of the two different AC-3 file playback scenarios on a Mac.
❶ Playback in QuickTime or DVD Player requires an external Decoder.
❷ Playback in Compressor utilizes the build in Decoder. However, it requires an Audio Interface that is connected to the surround speaker setup.
❸ The down-mix capability enables the playback through the stereo speakers.

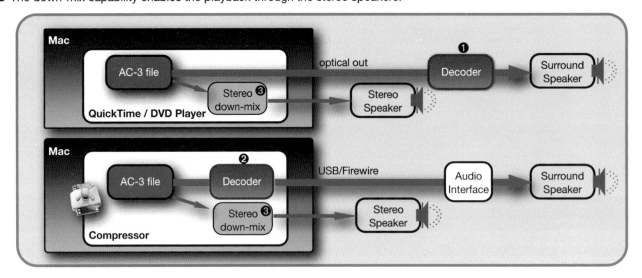

Render Farm

Why should we learn about render farms if we are not running Pixar Studios or any other big animation facility? Because that topic is not only relevant for the big guys but also for anybody using more than one computer on a local network. The good news is that all the required software comes with Compressor. However, trying to read up on the subject could be scary with all the specific lingo and technical terms.

Let me try to explain the topic in a way that hopefully makes you curious enough to realize that the whole subject is not so complicated after all. It is actually cool, once you've tried it and have your own little render farm up and running.

Distributed Processes

The first obstacle, as with many technologies, is the knowledge of the terminology. Clusters, Nodes, Services, Unmanaged Services, Shared Storage, etc. All that seems overwhelming. So let's start again with the basic understanding of the terms and basic concepts before opening any configuration page.

We talked a lot about processes, transcoding processes specifically. A process is nothing other than a fancy word for "work" or "stuff to do". After you've configured how you want to transcode (change) your Source Media File in Compressor, you hit the "Submit" button to start the actual Processing, or "the work". And who do you give the work to? - Most likely to the computer that you are working on. And how long does your computer "work" on the transcoding? - It depends. If there is little work to do and you have a powerful computer, then the work is done fairly quickly. However, if you have a lot of work to do, i.e. a two hour movie transcoded to a highly compressed output format, then the process could take hours even with a powerful machine. On top of that, while your computer is performing the process, you may be forced to pause whatever you are currently working on (i.e.FCPx editing).

This is were the concept of "Distributed Processes" comes in. Instead of having one worker digging out a hole, you hire 5 workers to dig the hole and it will be done much faster.

How about this analogy:

- Little Timmy comes home from school with five pages of math problems for his homework. Instead of doing them all by himself and working through the night he gives each of his four brothers one page, leaving him a single page to do.

- If he's smart, he'll give the fifth page to his sister, thereby distributing all the work to his siblings without doing any himself. This frees up his schedule to do more important things, like playing games.

- Staying with the same example. How about if one of Timmy's brothers is older and can finish the one page in no time, while the younger brother might take much longer. Timmy might give him less to do than his older brother. Same analogy with computers. You might distribute the processes to multiple computers, dividing up the work depending on the capabilities of the computers involved, i.e. a powerful MacPro that can perform more processing cycles than an older MacMini.

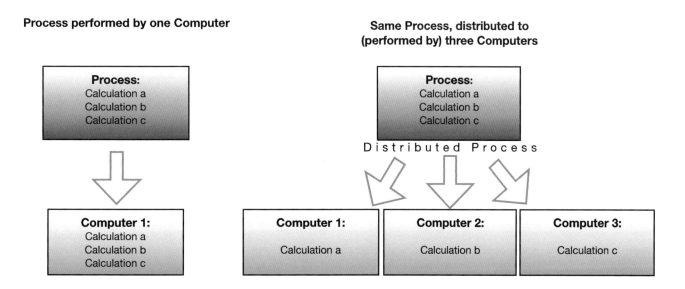

Now lets look at those examples with the right terminology:

▶ **Apple Qmaster**

Apple Qmaster is the name of the system that enables the whole Distributed Processing. Apple released the system in 2009 and the technology is used by Compressor and other applications like FCPx, Motion, Shake and DVD Studio Pro. Part of the confusion is that "Apple Qmaster" is the name of the distributed processing system but also the name of the application "Apple Qmaster", the client software used to submit Batches for processing.

▶ **Client**

The Client is the one that wants the work to be done and utilizes the Distributed Processing system to get that work done. In Timmy's example, that would be Timmy who wants his homework assignment done (as quickly as possible.). In our world a Client or Client Computer could be FCPx running on a machine that wants to export a Project using the distributed system. Or it could be Compressor, submitting a Batch to be transcoded (as quickly as possible) by using the distributed system.

▶ **Cluster**

A cluster is the group that processes the work. In Timmy's examples, that would be his siblings, helping him with his homework. In our world that would be a group of computers that are connected on a local network. The Client Computer can then send its "work" to that group of computers.

▶ **Service Node**

Each individual member in a Cluster that "accepts work" is called a Service Node or sometimes also referred to only as a *Node* or a *Service*. In Timmy's world that would be each one of the siblings that participates in the joint effort. In our world that would be each individual computer on the local network that can accept "work".

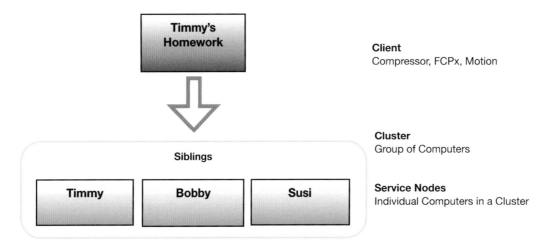

▶ **Cluster Controller**

The Cluster Controller acts as the manager for a specific cluster that distributes the processes within the cluster in the most efficient way. In Timmy's example that could be himself. He knows to give the younger sibling less work to do than the older brother. In computer terms, the Cluster Controller is a dedicated machine in a big system. In smaller Cluster configurations with less demanding wok, the function of the Cluster Controller can be assigned to one of the Service Node computers.

▶ **Shared Cluster Storage**

This is a directory (a dedicated folder) that functions as a central in-and-out box that all the machines in the Cluster must have access to. In Timmy's world that could be a basket in the kitchen where he puts the homework assignment. His brothers and sisters grab their part from there and put it back once they are finished with the work. Same principle in the computer world. Every computer in the Cluster must have access to a central storage location. That could be a dedicated storage solution in a big system, or just a folder on one of the participating Service Node machines.

Apple Qmaster System

Here is a quick look at the various components that make up the distributed process. They are all accessible conveniently from the Compressor app with a little bit of unusual interface implementation. Let me explain the basic layout.

There are four components involved.

❶ The Client Application:
This is the application that creates the work that needs processing. In our case it is the Compressor app that creates the Batch. Clients could also be FCP, Motion or other apps that support the Apple Qmaster System.

The next three components are each represented by a menu command under the Compressor's main menu *Apple Qmaster*:

❷ Configure the Computer to be part of the Distributed Processing

The command "*Share This Computer*" opens the window *Apple Qmaster Sharing*. With it's two tabs, it provides all the parameters to configure the individual computers to be used in a simple distributed processing setup. (Those settings were part of a separate System Preferences in Compressor3 but are now integrated in Compressor4.)

❸ Apple Qmaster

The command "*Create Rendering Jobs*" opens a separate application, *Apple Qmaster*. Please note, that this is a strange interface mechanism. You select a menu command in Compressor which opens a window in a different app that gets launched unnoticed in the background. Just looking at the Main Menu bar proves that the application has switched from Compressor to Apple Qmaster. The good news is that you might not need this command and the launched application at all if you just do basic rendering jobs in Compressor (only if you need the Apple Qmaster application as the client software to submit jobs and batches for Shake and other related software).

❹ Apple Qadministrator

The menu command "Administer Clusters" behaves in a similar way. You select it, a window opens, the application now switches to another app, "Apple Qadministrator". This app is for advanced Cluster configurations and can be ignored for simple Cluster setups.

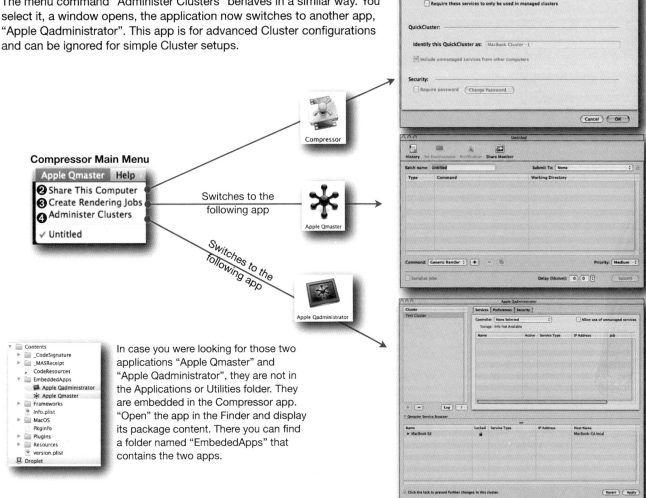

In case you were looking for those two applications "Apple Qmaster" and "Apple Qadministrator", they are not in the Applications or Utilities folder. They are embedded in the Compressor app. "Open" the app in the Finder and display its package content. There you can find a folder named "EmbededApps" that contains the two apps.

Cluster Setup

So how do you create or configure a Cluster?

First of all, you have to know that the Apple Qmaster system provides three different types of Cluster setups.

Easy Cluster Setup: *"This Computer Plus"*
Medium Cluster Setup: *"QuickCluster"*
Advanced Cluster Setup: *"Managed Cluster"*

We just learned the main components involved in a Cluster:

▶ Client
▶ Cluster
▶ Cluster Controller
▶ Service Node
▶ Shared Storage

Think of those components as "roles" in a Cluster Setup. These roles are assigned to computers in a Cluster Setup. And this marks the main difference between the three Cluster types. Deciding which of those software components (the roles) are running on what computer.

The example below shows the advanced type of a Cluster where each component is running on a dedicated machine.

➡ Advanced Cluster Setup: **Managed Cluster**

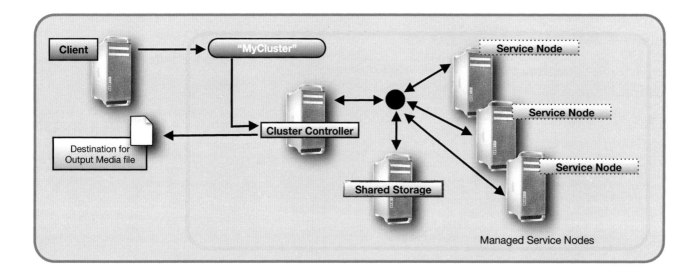

Example:

- A computer running the client software (i.e. Compressor) that sends its Job to a specific Cluster. That Cluster with the name "MyCluster" has been configured earlier as part of the Apple Qmaster System and its name shows up in the Compressor's Submit window as an available processing option.

- The *MyCluster* has a dedicated computer running the Cluster Controller which manages the distribution of the processing among the available Service Nodes.

- The *MyCluster* example has three dedicated machines that run as Service Nodes. They are called "Managed Services" because they are part of the configured *MyCluster*, controlled by its Cluster Controller.

- A separate Computer or a network storage device functions as the Shared Cluster Storage where each Service Node reads and writes their portion of the processing job.

- The Cluster Controller then puts all those individual elements from the Service Nodes together and saves the finished job at the end to the Destination that was described in the original "Job Description" by the Client.

➡ Medium Cluster Setup: **QuickCluster**

This type of a Cluster also has all the main components but with two major differences:

▸ The Cluster is represented by only one machine that runs the Cluster Controller, functions as a Service Node and provides the Shared Storage. This so called "QuickCluster" is therefore a Cluster made up of only one computer. However, this easy to configure Cluster (hence the name "QuickCluster") is enough to let a Client Computer distribute ("hand over") its Job to this QuickCluster and let it do the work, freeing up its own CPU cycles.

▸ The second difference compared to the Advanced Cluster Setup is the treatment of Service Nodes. The QuickCluster can also make use of additional Service Nodes on the network (as an option). These are the Computers that are configured to make their Service available in an Apple Qmaster distributed processing system. They are called "unmanaged Service Nodes" because they are not part of a dedicated Cluster configuration.

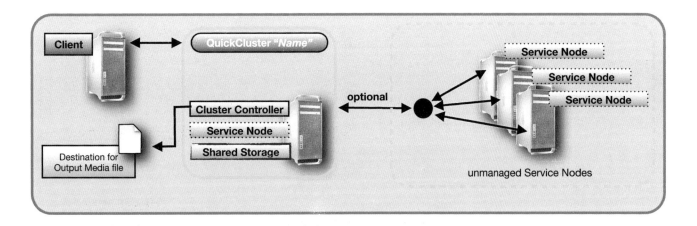

➡ Easy Cluster Setup: **This Computer Plus**

This is the quickest way to take advantage of the Distributed Processing System without the need of complicated Cluster configurations. It involves only two parts:

▸ As you can see in the illustration, there is technically no Cluster involved at all. The Computer that runs the Client also includes the functionality of the Cluster Controller, the Service Node and the Shared Storage.

▸ However, if the process would only run on the Client Computer (*This Computer*), then there would be no process distributed. That's where the "Plus" comes in. The Cluster Controller, running on This Computer, is looking on the network for unmanaged Service Nodes. These are Computers that are configured to make their Service available in an Apple Qmaster distributed processing system (the same kind of machines that a QuickCluster makes use of). If it finds any Service Nodes, then it automatically distributes the processes between **This Computer "plus"** any of those unmanaged Service Nodes.

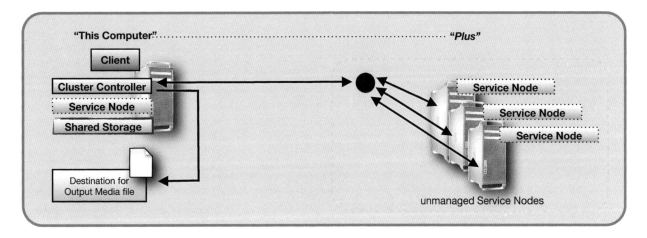

"Do the processing on This Computer (the Client), PLUS look for other computers on the network that offer their Services".

And finally, with all that knowledge and understanding, lets look at how to configure and use those Clusters:

 This Computer Plus - Setup

▶ **Use the Cluster**

"This Computer Plus" is available in Compressor, FCPx and Motion. Whenever you start a process (export, batch, etc) look for the "This Computer Plus" option.

- **In Compressor**: When you click the Submit button, a dialog window opens up. "This Computer" is the default selection from the *Cluster* popup menu. This setting would use only the current computer for the processing. Now select the checkbox "This Computer Plus" to extend the processing to all the computers on the network that offer their services.

- **In FCPx or Motion**: Most of the export options in the Share Menu display a configuration window with an "Advanced" tab. This provides the settings for Background Rendering. Select "*This Computer Plus*" from the popup menu.

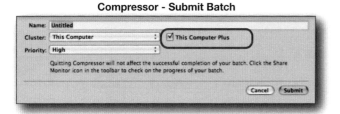
Compressor - Submit Batch

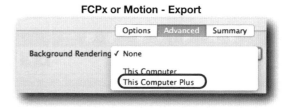
FCPx or Motion - Export

That's the reason why this type of distributed processing is so simple. From the Client side, you only have to select this option, which is always there. Once selected, the system automatically looks for any computer that offers Services and includes those computers in the joint processing. However, you have to configure those computers first. The good news is that this is very simple:

▶ **Configure the Cluster**

Actually, you don't have to configure the Cluster, only the Service Nodes. Each computer that you want to use as a Service Node for distributed processing requires the following setup:

- Install Compressor on the machine first.
- Open the Apple Qmaster Sharing window with the Compressor's Main Menu command *Apple Qmaster > Share This Computer > Setup*
- Check the "Share this computer" checkbox and select the "*as Services only*" radio button. This makes this machine a Service Node, ready to accept processing jobs.
- In the next section of the window under Services, check the "*Compressor*" checkbox. The *Options* button opens a window that displays the "Number of Instances", or in other words, the number of cores for the computer's CPU. The popup menu lets you select how many of the cores you want to make available. Please note that more is not always better. It depends on the available RAM. The selected number of Instances shouldn't be bigger than "2 x the available RAM".
- Leave the other checkboxes unchecked (they might be grayed out anyways). Leave the other settings in the Advanced tab as their default.

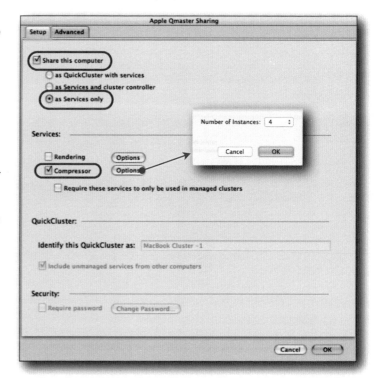

▶ **Use the Cluster:**

This Cluster type is also available in Compressor, FCPx and Motion.

- **In Compressor**: When you click the Submit button, a dialog window opens up. "This Computer" is the default selection from the *Cluster* popup menu. The popup menu lists any configured Clusters, Managed Clusters or QuickClusters. In the example below, "MacBook Cluster" is a configured QuickCluster on that Network. Selecting it will use it as the distributed processing system.

- **In FCPx or Motion**: Most of the export options in the Share Menu display a configuration window with an "Advanced" tab. This provides the settings for Background Rendering. The popup menu lists any configured Clusters, Managed Clusters or QuickClusters. In the example below, "MacBook Cluster" is a configured QuickCluster on that Network. Selecting it will use it as the distributed processing system.

Compressor - Submit Batch

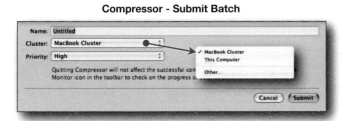

FCPx or Motion - Export

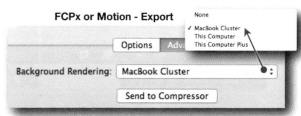

▶ **Configure the Cluster**

The configuration for the QuickCluster involves two parts: The Cluster itself and the Service Nodes.

- First install Compressor on the machine that you want to use as the QuickCluster.

- Open the Apple Qmaster Sharing window with the Compressor's Main Menu command
  Apple Qmaster > Share This Computer > Setup

- ❶ Check the "Share this computer" checkbox and select the "*as QuickCluster with services*" radio button. That will configure this Machine as the QuickCluster.

- ❷ In the next section of the window under Services, check the "*Compressor*" checkbox. The Options button opens a window that displays the "Number of Instances", or in other words, the number of cores for the computer's CPU. The popup menu lets you select how many of the cores you want to make available. Please note that more is not always better. It depends on the available RAM. The selected number of Instances shouldn't be bigger than "2 x the available RAM".

- ❸ In the next section under QuickCluster, enter a name or keep the default name. This is the name that will be displayed in the Cluster popup menu when you submit a batch. In this example "MacBook Cluster". Check the box below to "include unmanaged services from other computers. This will enable the Cluster to look for other unmanaged Service Nodes on the Network to be included in the distributed process.

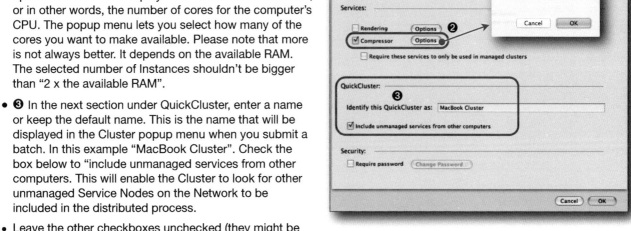

- Leave the other checkboxes unchecked (they might be grayed out anyways). Leave the other settings in the Advanced tab as their default.

Now if you want to include other computers as Service Nodes as part of the distributed process, you have to configure those machines as Service Nodes. The configuration is the same as with "This Computer Plus", described on the previous page.

Managed Cluster - Setup

The configuration of a Managed Cluster is more complex and requires the Apple Qadministrator app. It launches from the Compressor Main Menu *Apple Qmaster > Administer Clusters*.

This is for more demanding processing environments that require configurations by system admins. I don't want to get into that territory and will leave it to the official Apple documentation which provides more information.

Miscellaneous Configurations

The Advanced tab of the Apple Qmaster Sharing window has a few additional settings:

- Restart the services every 24 hours or create a specific schedule on the Service Schedule window.
- Manage the Shared Cluster Storage. Define a location and the time to reset the folder. This is the default Destination "*Cluster Storage*" that is available in the Destinations Window.
- Manage Network Configuration.
- Manage Log files.
- Set a name for the computer as a Cluster Identifier.

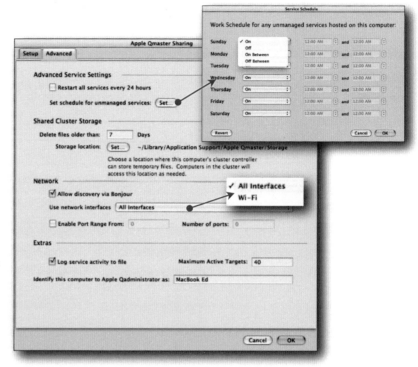

Mixed Environment

Once you configured your Clusters and Service Nodes, any Client Computer on your network can access them. That means that more than one Client can use them. This is similar to a network printer where any computer on the network can use that printer.

Share Monitor

And similar to a network printer, all the different jobs that are sent to that printer will end up in a queue and the printer software (or in our case the Cluster Controller) will process those jobs.

The progress of the processes can be monitored in the Share Monitor app. It will display the individual progress on each Service Node, which job is done, which one is in queue and which one is in progress. This gives you a nice overview when a lot of jobs are processed at the same time.

Copy Source Media file to Cluster

There is one important decision you have to make when you use a Cluster setup: What should happen with the Source Media file of a Job.

Usually it is located on the Client computer. If you want to move the processing over to a separate Cluster computer, you also might want to move the Source Media file to the Cluster (Shared Cluster Storage). Otherwise the Service Nodes have to constantly read the Source file data from the Client computer, constantly "bothering" your Client computer while you might want to continue with other tasks.

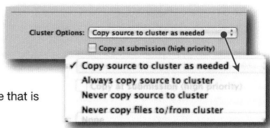

However if the Source Media file is a couple of Gigabytes big, then the time that is needed for the Cluster Controller to copy the file over would beat the time advantage of the distributed processing.

Compressor lets you choose what fits your needs the best. The Preference window provides a popup menu with the different Cluster Options.

Conclusion

This concludes my "*Compressor 4 - How it Works*" manual. I hope I've helped you to understand this small but powerful app.

Other titles available in my series of Graphically Enhance Manuals are:

- Final Cut Pro X - How it Works (also available in German)
- Final Cut Pro X - The Details (also available in German)
- Motion 5 - How it Works (release date April 2012)

If you find my visual approach of explaining topics and concepts helpful, please recommend my books to others or write a review on Amazon on one of my product pages. This will help me to continue this series.

Special thanks to my beautiful wife Li and my son Winston for their love and understanding during the long hours of working on the book.

I'd like to dedicate this book to my brother Helmut who lost his battle with cancer while I was writing this book. I miss you a lot.

You can find more of my Graphically Enhanced Manuals on my website at:

www.DingDingMusic.com/GEM

There is also information about my day job as a composer and links to follow me on my social network sites:

www.DingDingMusic.com

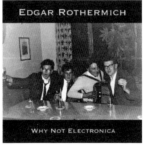

To contact me directly, email me at:

GEM@DingDingMusic.com

Thanks for you interest and your support,

Edgar Rothermich

Made in the USA
Lexington, KY
07 May 2012